LAVENDER L·I·S·T·S

New lists about lesbian and gay culture, history, and personalities

by Lynne Yamaguchi Fletcher
and Adrien Saks

BOSTON • ALYSON PUBLICATIONS, INC.

Portraits of Anna Dickenson and Margaret Fuller
are reproduced from the *Dictionary of American Portraits,*
published by Dover Publications, Inc., 1967.

Published as a trade paperback original by Alyson Publications, Inc.,
40 Plympton St., Boston, Mass. 02118
Distributed in England by GMP Publishers,
P.O. Box 247, London N17 9QR England.

First edition, first printing: December 1990

ISBN 1-55583-182-6

LAVENDER LISTS

CONTENTS

From whence we came, 81

Mightier than the sword, 117

Daring to speak our name, 151

Making our way, 175

The spice of life, 201

To all you who by your example or your endeavors
show the world that gays and lesbians are,
and long have been,
a vital part of humanity

&
to Cath,
for loving me,
and to the whole animal family

—lyf

INTRODUCTION

This addition to the growing library of "list" books is intended for both lesbians and gay men. In it we have tried to emphasize our common culture and history, and to present a balance of information of interest to lesbians and gays. We've done a fair job, we think, though we have not been able to entirely avoid a male bias: History is still "his story," and sexism still largely determines whose story and what events are considered newsworthy — even in gay resources. Fully countering the bias would have required research time that we regrettably did not have, as well as resources that don't yet exist.

You'll find that the lists presented here span history to the present. They are not comprehensive, however; they are not meant to be. We mean to amuse, not instruct — though we certainly hope readers will learn along the way. Some items we left out because we simply didn't have enough information about them. Where items were quite similar, we chose the most interesting or most representative. We also left out entries that would have duplicated information included in *The Gay Book of Lists, Lesbian Lists,* or *The Gay Fireside Companion,* so if you see major omissions, look there before chiding us.

Though only two names appear as authors on the cover, this book is in your hands only through the efforts of many others. We especially thank Sasha Alyson for creating the opportunity for us to work on this project and for his invaluable hands-on assistance every step of the way. And we thank Karen Barber for the hours she spent at a copy machine on our behalf, for her diligence in tracking down stray details, and for her generous support throughout the chaos.

Thanks also go to those mentioned in individual lists, as well as to Leigh Rutledge, Eric Garber, Joan Nestle, the Lesbian Herstory Archives, the Lambda Legal Defense and Education Fund, the National Gay and Lesbian Task Force, Helaine Harris, Kate

Dyer, Barbara Grier, Richard Burns, Michael Denneny and Keith Kahla, and Thomas W Schloeder. We would also like to acknowledge our indebtedness to *The Advocate* — all twenty-some years' worth of issues — and to the *Encyclopedia of Homosexuality,* edited by Wayne R. Dynes, as primary sources of information.

Putting this book together has been an adventure for both of us. We have learned more — trivial and significant — than we ever imagined we'd have call to know about what being lesbian or gay has meant — in our time and culture as well as historically and cross-culturally. Adrien will never get over the fact that in September 1969 *The Advocate* devoted its front page to the Groovy Guy Contest — relegating its first coverage of the Stonewall Riot to page 3. Lynne suspects more than ever that, in this culture at least, the one thing lesbians and gay men really have in common is the way we've been treated by the straight world. We both hope that, gay man or lesbian, you will find in these pages an adventure of your own.

Lynne Yamaguchi Fletcher
& Adrien Saks

LAVENDER LISTS

An Army of Lovers

It was Anna Dickenson's oral skills that first attracted Susan B. Anthony.

16 COUPLES AND HOW THEY MET

1. SUSAN B. ANTHONY and ANNA DICKENSON

Anthony was for many years active in both the abolitionist and suffrage movements. One day she went to hear a new anti-slavery orator who, though only twenty, had already developed powerful speaking skills. The orator was Anna Dickenson, and after hearing her speak, Anthony reported that she felt "fully repaid for all the years of odium through which we have passed in order to make it possible for women to speak on the political topics of the day." A long and close relationship followed.

2. EMILY DICKINSON and SUSAN GILBERT

Susan Gilbert was orphaned at the age of eleven, and spent her early teenage years living in several families. She traveled extensively, and soon developed into an outgoing, colorful, and mature young woman.

Gilbert and Dickinson met when they were both sixteen, as students at Amherst Academy in central Massachusetts. Emily was instantly taken with Sue. In the years to come, her letters home would be full of excited and gushing references to her new friend.

3. OSCAR WILDE and LORD ALFRED DOUGLAS

The spoiled, insolent, and charming young Lord Douglas was given a copy of *The Picture of Dorian Gray* by his cousin. He reportedly read it "fourteen times running," then arranged to meet the author.

From that point, accounts differ. Douglas insisted that Wilde was instantly infatuated, and wooed him for the next six months. Wilde denied that — though he may have been wooing so many young men at the time that he lost track. According to Wilde, the relationship only solidified because Douglas, under threat of blackmail when an indiscreet letter fell into the wrong hands, came to him for help. The incriminating letter was easily, though not inexpensively, purchased from the blackmailer, and for a time, the Wilde–Douglas affair flourished.

4. RADCLYFFE HALL and VERONICA (MABEL) BATTEN

Hall and Batten met at Homburg, a German spa that the fifty-year-old Batten was visiting in hopes of easing her health problems. Hall fell in love immediately and established a friendship with the older woman; a year later, while traveling together, they became lovers.

5. RADCLYFFE HALL and LADY TROUBRIDGE

In the early months of World War I, the young Una Troubridge was trying to raise funds for a naval hospital, but with only limited success. Depressed, she went to visit her cousin, Lady Clarendon.

Meanwhile Radclyffe Hall, then 35, was living with the ailing 58-year-old Mabel Batten — Lady Clarendon's sister. When Lady Troubridge arrived for her visit, she met Hall and Batten in the Clarendon drawing room. Both Hall and Troubridge felt an immediate connection that developed into a full-fledged love affair.

Gertrude Stein and Alice B. Toklas couldn't agree on which of them fell in love with the other first, but love it was, for thirty-nine years.

6. GERTRUDE STEIN and ALICE B. TOKLAS

Alice B. Toklas was visiting the Stein family in Paris when Gertrude entered the room, freshly back from a summer in Italy. According to Gertrude (years later), Alice heard bells on that first meeting. Alice reported that Gertrude had fallen in love at first sight. In any event, they spent their first evening together, in that fall of 1907, at a cafe off the boulevard Saint-Michel, eating praline ices.

7. NATALIE BARNEY and ROMAINE BROOKS

Brooks, an American painter living in Paris, was introduced to Barney in 1915 at a tea party given by an American heiress who had married an English lord and moved to Paris. What is interesting is not how they met, but that it took so long. The two women had been living in Paris, and moving in the same crowd of wealthy international socialites, for ten years before they said their first *bonjour* to one another. The relationship lasted fifty-five years, but broke up when the two women were both in their nineties.

Sometimes a hat is a useful accessory: Sylvia Beach and Adrienne Monnier at Shakespeare and Company in 1935.

8. SYLVIA BEACH and ADRIENNE MONNIER

It was a blustering March day in 1917. Adrienne Monnier was a young French writer and publisher who also operated her own Left Bank bookshop in Paris. When a shy young American woman walked into the shop, Monnier did her best to make the newcomer feel welcome, and they had a long talk about literature and language.

As Beach was leaving, a gust of wind blew her hat into the middle of the street. Adrienne ran out to rescue it. She returned it to Sylvia, the two women's eyes met, and they laughed. Within two years, Beach had taken up permanent residency in Paris and opened her own store across the street.

9. BRYHER and H.D.

Bryher, who adopted the name of one of her beloved Scilly Islands as her own, was twenty-four when she read the work of H.D. and decided she must meet this wonderful poet. She wrote and asked permission to visit. H.D. thought the letter seemed to have been written by an elderly schoolteacher, and issued an invitation.

Clyde Tolson (left) rose "solely on merit" to his spot by J. Edgar Hoover's side. (1942)

On July 17, 1918, Bryher arrived at H.D.'s home in Cornwall. She later recalled, perhaps with some poetic license, that H.D.'s first words were, "I was waiting for you to come." Bryher quickly invited H.D. to travel with her to the Scillies, and a romance began.

10. J. EDGAR HOOVER and CLYDE TOLSON

For four years, from 1924 to 1928, FBI director J. Edgar Hoover gave rapid promotions and salary raises to his handsome associate and friend, T. Frank Baughman.

In 1928, the equally handsome Clyde Tolson started working as an FBI special agent. So far as is known, this was the first time he and Hoover had met. Soon Tolson was the new rising star in the bureau, and Baughman's position plunged. Within two years, Tolson was the bureau's assistant director, and Hoover told a reporter, "I hardly recall any case where a man has risen solely on merit with such rapidity."

Hoover and Tolson, both bachelors, lunched together every day for the rest of their lives and spent much of their off-work time together. After his death, Hoover was found to have kept hundreds of photographs of Tolson from their 42-year friendship.

11. ELEANOR ROOSEVELT and LORENA HICKOCK
The country was in a depression. Franklin Roosevelt was in a close battle to win the Democratic nomination for president. Eleanor Roosevelt, who emphatically did not want to live in the White House, had nonetheless invited a group of women reporters to the Roosevelt mansion. She was scrambling eggs when Lorena Hickock first saw her.

Roosevelt admired the fact that Hickock had become a high-ranking reporter in a profession dominated by men. By election day, they had become close friends.

12. DEL MARTIN and PHYLLIS LYON
The two long-time lesbian activists met on the job in Seattle, Washington. In 1949 they both worked for a publisher in the building and engineering industry. Del was editing daily construction reports; Phyllis was associate editor of the weekly construction news and the monthly *Pacific Builder and Engineer.* In 1953, Phyllis started making plans to move out of town. "Until then, I had just considered her my straight friend," recalls Del. "That's when I made my move." Two years later, as lovers, Martin and Lyon co-founded the Daughters of Bilitis, the nation's first lesbian organization, and have played a prominent role in it ever since.

13. CHRISTOPHER ISHERWOOD and DON BACHARDY
The already-famous writer and later-to-be-famous artist met at a party in 1953. Isherwood was 48; Bachardy, 18. "We all drank a lot — which I almost never did, in those days — and at the end of it Chris and I kissed and hugged each other and lost our balance and fell right through a window," Bachardy recalled many years later. "We didn't see each other for two months, but it had sort of broken the ice. When we met again, we weren't strangers." Bachardy takes credit for having made the first move: "I think the younger one usually has to, in a case like that. Older people are so shy."

14. BARBARA GRIER and DONNA McBRIDE

Naiad Press publisher and former *Ladder* editor Barbara Grier met her first lover in 1952 in the literature department of the Kansas City (Mo.) Public Library. Grier was nineteen. Not long afterward, accompanied by Grier's mother, the two women headed for Denver, where they spent twenty years together.

Not long after that relationship ended, Grier returned to the same department of the same library. There she met Donna McBride; they have been together ever since.

McBride took an administrative position at the library soon after they met, and abolished the Literature department. She thus ensured, says Grier, "that I cannot go shopping there again in 1992, when we will have been together 20 years."

15. MARK THOMPSON and MALCOLM BOYD

Mark Thompson, longtime senior editor at *The Advocate,* says that he and Malcolm Boyd began their relationship "the old-fashioned way." Mark was in Los Angeles in February of 1984. He returned to the gay hotel where he was staying, "hot and tired and ready to relax," and found a note from a friend saying that Malcolm Boyd was staying at the same hotel; could they get together?

"I was really tired and didn't feel like it, but this was a close mutual friend," recalls Mark, so he dropped by for a quick hello. That turned into a three-hour talk, then Mark flew back to San Francisco, not expecting to see Malcolm again. But a few months later *The Advocate* moved from northern California to L.A. The two men went to a small restaurant in the conservative suburb of Pasadena where, being from San Francisco, Mark thought nothing of dancing with Malcolm. "That cleared the restaurant out pretty fast," he remembers. A two-year courtship followed; after which Malcolm took Mark to a restaurant, gave him a ring, and proposed.

16. THE REV. TROY PERRY and PHILLIP RAY DeBLICK

They first briefly met — where else? — in church, but Perry soon forgot that encounter. Two years later, they were both in a local leather bar, and their eyes met from across the room. "We

Who could resist her? Natalie Barney as a young woman.

exchanged phone numbers," Troy says, "and two weeks later we had our first date and he never went home."

17 LOVERS OF NATALIE BARNEY

According to biographer George Wickes, Natalie Barney once compiled a list of "liaisons and 'demi-liaisons'" that included "some forty names and omit[ted] casual affairs without number." And her first book, *Quelques portraits-sonnets de femmes*, published in her early twenties, contains thirty-four poems, addressed to some two dozen different women. From her biography, we glean the following:

1. EVALINA "EVA" PALMER, her first love, who "initiated Natalie into the rites of Lesbos"

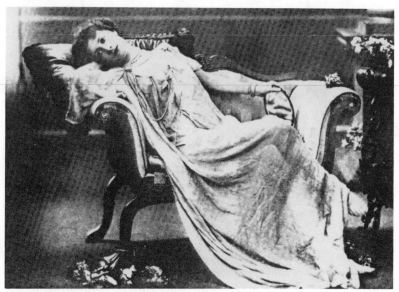

Succumbing to the heat? Liane de Pougy in the summer of 1899.

2. AN UNIDENTIFIED SPANISH WOMAN

3. LIANE DE POUGY, a famous courtesan who wrote of her love affair with Barney in a sensational novel, *Idylle saphique,* published in 1901

4. RENEÉ VIVIEN (PAULINE TARN), Barney's first "great love"

5. "AN ACTRESS WITH GOLDEN EYES"

6. LUCIE DELARUE-MARDRUS, a writer and the wife of a doctor and "Orientalist"; she fictionalized Barney in a novel and wrote passionate love poems to her, published posthumously in *Nos Secrótes Amours*

7. COLETTE, whose "demi-liaison" with Barney became a lifetime friendship

8. HENRIETTE ROGGERS, an actress

9. AN UNNAMED ACTRESS whom Barney pursued to Saint Petersburg only to be met by a Russian colonel and French diplomat

10. ELISABETH "LILY" DE GRAMONT, DUCHESS DE CLERMONT-TONNERE, lovers with Barney for several years, and one of her dearest friends till her death

11. THE BARONESS DESLANDES

12. ARMEN OHANIAN, a Persian dancer

13. ROMAINE BROOKS, an American painter and one of the great loves of Barney's life; their relationship lasted fifty-five years, only to end over Barney's unceasing infidelity

14. CECILE SARTORIS, translator of a novel by Remy de Gourmont

15. DOLLY WILDE, niece of Oscar Wilde

16. NADINE HOANG, a Chinese lawyer who fought as a man in the Chinese army for four years

17. JANINE LOHAVARY, the hitherto straight wife of a retired ambassador, and the straw that broke Romaine Brooks's back; Lohavary stayed with Barney till her death in 1972

10 MARRIAGES THAT MUST HAVE REQUIRED SOME EXTRA EFFORT

1. Bisexual writer CARSON McCULLERS and gay REEVES McCULLERS, who simultaneously had an affair with the same man

2. Poet BRYHER (more lesbian than straight) and writer ROBERT McALMON (gay)

3. Poet H.D. (Bryher's lesbian lover) and writer RICHARD ALDINGTON (straight)

4. Actress KATHARINE CORNELL and producer GUTHRIE McCLINTIC, both bisexual, in a very open marriage

5. Writer KATHERINE MANSFIELD, who had a lifelong relationship with Ida Constance Baker, and writer and editor JOHN MIDDLETON MURRY (straight)

6. Writer VITA SACKVILLE-WEST and writer and diplomat HAROLD NICOLSON (both bisexual)

7. Writer VIOLET KEPPEL (Vita Sackville-West's lover) and DENYS TREFUSIS (himself gay)

8. Sexual psychologist HAVELOCK ELLIS and lesbian EDITH LEES

9. ROMAINE GODDARD BROOKS, lifelong love of Natalie Barney, and homosexual pianist JOHN ELLINGHAM BROOKS

10. The bisexual American writer and composer PAUL BOWLES and JANE AUER BOWLES, a "very promiscuous" lesbian and later a well-known fiction writer

54 PEOPLE WHO HAD RELATIONSHIPS WITH BOTH SEXES

1. ALEXANDER THE GREAT (356–323 B.C.), *ruler*

2. SAINT AUGUSTINE (343–430), *theologian*

3. JOSEPHINE BAKER (1906–1975), *entertainer*

4. TALLULAH BANKHEAD (1902–1968), *actress*

5. DJUNA BARNES (1892–1982), *novelist*

6. DAVID BOWIE (1947–), *musician*

7. JANE BOWLES (1917–1973), *writer*

8. BRYHER (1894–1983), *poet*

9. LORD BYRON (1788–1824), *poet*

10. CALIGULA (A.D.12–41), *tyrant*

Margaret Fuller, the early feminist activist, saw same-sex love as far superior to heterosexuality. "It is purely intellectual and spiritual, unprofaned by any mixture of lower instincts, undisturbed by any need of consulting temporal interests," she wrote in her journals.

11. JULIUS CAESAR (100–44 B.C.), *ruler*

12. JOHN CHEEVER (1912–1982), *writer*

13. COLETTE (1873–1954), *novelist*

14. KATHARINE CORNELL (1893–1974), *actress*

15. COUNTEE CULLEN (1903–1946), *poet*

16. JAMES DEAN (1931–1955), *actor*

17. SAMUEL DELANY (1942–   ), *novelist*

18. EMILY DICKINSON (1830–1886), *poet*

19. HAVELOCK ELLIS (1859–1939), *early sexologist*

20. ERROL FLYNN (1909–1959), *actor*

21. MARGARET FULLER (1810–1850), *early feminist*

22. PAUL GOODMAN (1911–1972), *writer*

23. LORRAINE HANSBERRY (1930–1965), *playwright*

24. LANGSTON HUGHES (1902–1967), *poet*

25. ELTON JOHN (1947–), *rock star*

26. JANIS JOPLIN (1943–1970), *rock star*

27. JOHN MAYNARD KEYNES (1883–1946), *economist*

28. BILLIE JEAN KING (1943–), *athlete*

29. KATHERINE MANSFIELD (1888–1923), *writer*

30. W. SOMERSET MAUGHAM (1874–1965), *novelist*

31. CARSON McCULLERS (1917–1967), *novelist*

32. ROD McKUEN (1933–), *poet*

33. KATE MILLETT (1934–), *writer and activist*

34. YUKIO MISHIMA (1925–1970), *writer*

35. MARTINA NAVRATILOVA (1956–), *athlete*

36. VASLAV NIJINSKY (1890–1950), *dancer*

37. ANAIS NIN (1903–1977), *writer*

38. PHILLIP OF MACEDON (382–336 B.C.), *king*

39. TYRONE POWER (1914–1958), *actor*

40. PU YI (1906–1967), *emperor*

41. MA RAINEY (1886–1939), *singer*

42. VITA SACKVILLE-WEST (1892–1962), *writer*

43. MARQUIS DE SADE (1740–1814), *sadist*

44. PETER TCHAIKOVSKY (1840–1893), *composer*

45. SARA TEASDALE (1884–1933), *poet*

46. DOROTHY THOMPSON (1893–1961), *journalist*

47. RUDOLPH VALENTINO (1895–1926), *actor*

48. CARL VAN VECHTEN (1880–1964), *photographer*

A leading man to more than ladies: Rudolph Valentino, shown here in *Son of the Sheik.*

49. PAUL VERLAINE (1844–1896), *poet*

50. GORE VIDAL (1925–   ), *writer*

51. VOLTAIRE (1694–1778), *writer*

52. OSCAR WILDE (1854–1900), *playwright*

53. MARY WOLLSTONECRAFT (1759–1797), *writer*

54. VIRGINIA WOOLF (1882–1941), *writer*

11 GAY OR LESBIAN COUPLES IN BUSINESS TOGETHER

1. CAT CHASE and CONNIE MEREDITH
   These two lesbian bodybuilders opened South End Gym, a powerlifting workout facility in Boston, in 1985.

2. HANNS EBENSTEN and BRIAN KENNY
Partners for 27 years as of 1988, Ebensten and Kenny's travel company, Hanns Ebensten Travel, Inc., based in Key West, Florida, is one of the world's most successful gay-targeted businesses.

3. GRACE NEWMAN and JUDI HALL
Once a computer programmer and an administrator of a social services agency, Newman and Hall now own and run the Highlands Inn in New Hampshire.

4. DAVID McWHIRTER and ANDREW MATTISON
Psychiatrist McWhirter and psychologist Mattison are partners (along with five other therapists) in San Diego's Clinical Institute for Human Relationships and collaborators in a study of male homosexual couples (see p. 34).

5. EVIN EVANS and EMILY DAVIS
A couple since 1977, Evans and Davis operate a small goat farm in South Carolina, making and marketing their own goat cheese.

6. GARY NARGANG and FRANK CELIA
Lovers for thirteen years, Nargang and Celia raise turkeys together in California.

7. TOM NELSON and TIM BROWNE
Together since 1977, Nelson, formerly an insurance under-writer, and Browne, a clinical psychologist, now run and partially own the Oasis Guest House in Key West, Florida.

8. MARTINA NAVRATILOVA and JUDY NELSON
Nelson has designed the line of tennis clothes slated to be marketed under Navratilova's name.

9. EDITH SOMERVILLE and VIOLET MARTIN
Second cousins and inseparable companions for more than thirty years, this pair of Irish writers wrote fifteen books of fiction

together. The pair continued their collaboration even after Martin died in 1915: Edith Somerville wrote sixteen more books while in spiritual communication with her beloved Violet.

10. MARGARET ANDERSON (1886–1973) and JANE HEAP
Together these two lovers edited the *Little Review* (1915–1927), one of the best literary magazines of its time.

11. ANNA YEVREINOVA (1844–1919) and MARIA FEODOROVA
These Russian lovers jointly edited a literary journal called the *Northern Herald,* founded by Yevreinova.

13 PARENTS OF THE PAST

1. JOSEPHINE BAKER (1906–1975), *entertainer*

2. HENRY WARD BEECHER (1813–1887), *minister*

3. JOHN CHEEVER (1912–1982), *novelist*

4. MALCOLM FORBES (1919–1990), *financial publisher*

5. STEPHEN FOSTER (1826–1864), *composer*

6. PAUL GOODMAN (1911–1972), *writer*

7. JUAN II of Castile (1405–1454), *king*

8. THOMAS MANN (1875–1955), *novelist*

9. W. SOMERSET MAUGHAM (1874–1965), *writer*

10. ELEANOR ROOSEVELT (1884–1962), *humanitarian*

11. VITA SACKVILLE-WEST (1892–1962), *writer*

12. Dr. TOM WADDELL (1937–1987), *founder of the Gay Games*

13. MARY WOLLSTONECRAFT (1759–1797), *writer*

Mary Wollstonecraft named her first daughter, born out of wedlock in 1794, after Fanny Blood, the love of her life. She later died giving birth to a second daughter, Mary.

...AND 22 PARENTS OF THE PRESENT

1. ANN BANNON, *1950s lesbian "pulp" writer*

2. SUSIE BRIGHT, On Our Backs *editor, also known as Susie Sexpert*

3 & 4. DEBRA CHASNOFF and KIM KLAUSNER, *founding editors of* Out/Look *magazine*

5. PHYLLIS CHESLER, *writer*

6. DON CLARK, *psychologist and writer*

7. SAMUEL DELANY, *science-fiction writer*

8. JUDY GRAHN, *writer*

9. JAN GROVER, *editor of* Out/Look *magazine*

10. HARRY HAY, *activist and founder of the Mattachine Society*

11. DONNA HITCHENS, *California Supreme Court justice*

12. BILLY JONES, *black gay activist*

13. AUDRE LORDE, *writer*

14 & 15. DEL MARTIN and PHYLLIS LYON, *activists and writers*

16. SUSAN McGRIEVEY, *attorney and activist*

17. ROD McKUEN, *poet*

18. LORENZO WILSON MILAM, *author of* The Cripple Liberation Front Marching Band Blues

19. ROBIN MORGAN, *editor of* MS *magazine*

20. KAY OSTBERG, *lesbian activist; co-chair of the 1987 March on Washington*

21. MINNIE BRUCE PRATT, *poet*

22. ADRIENNE RICH, *writer*

7 THINGS THAT CHARLES HIX SAYS ARE SEXY ON MEN

1. THE COLOR RED

2. DRAWSTRING PANTS

3. PLAIN WHITE JOCKEY SHORTS

4. VISIBLE ZIPPERS

5. A TURNED-DOWN WAISTBAND ON GYM SHORTS

6. PANTS THAT CONTOUR THE BUTTOCKS

7. SPONTANEITY (as opposed to "a heavy-handed attempt to look sexy")

6 STAGES IN A GAY MALE RELATIONSHIP

These stages, and their characteristics, are identified and described by David P. McWhirter and Andrew M. Mattison in their book *The Male Couple.*

1. BLENDING (first year)
   Merging of two personalities
   Limerence (a feeling of being in love)
   High sexual activity
   Equalizing of partnership

2. NESTING (second and third years)
   Attention to making an attractive and comfortable home
   Finding compatibility and resolving differences
   A decline of limerence
   Ambivalence about the relationship

3. MAINTAINING (fourth and fifth years)
   Reappearance of individuality
   An increased willingness to take risks and express negative feelings
   Learning to deal with conflict with one another
   Establishing traditions

4. BUILDING (sixth through tenth years)
   Better collaborating to reach shared goals
   Increasing productivity in other endeavors, as maintenance of the relationship consumes less time
   Establishing independence, including separate friendships, and sometimes outside sexual relationships
   A decline in sexual attraction as familiarity grows

5. RELEASING (eleventh through twentieth years)
   Trusting and accepting the other person as he is
   Merging of money and possessions

Constricting of the relationship, and decreasing contacts with
   the outside world
Taking one another for granted

6. RENEWING (beyond twenty years)
   Wanting, and achieving, a sense of security
   Shifting perspectives, as each person ages
   Frequent reminiscing

10 TOP CONDOMS, AS RATED BY CONSUMER REPORTS

In 1989, *Consumer Reports* magazine rated 40 widely available
brands and models of condoms to see which were most likely to
fail in use. The top ten, from best to worst, were:

1. Gold Circle Coin

2. LifeStyles Extra Strength Lubricated

3. Saxon Wet Lubricated

4. Ramses Non-Lubricated Reservoir end

5. Sheik Non-Lubricated Reservoir End

6. Excita Extra

7. Kimono

8. Sheik Elite

9. Koromex with Nonoxynol-9

10. Excita Fiesta

...AND 8 CONDOMS MOST LIKELY TO FAIL
(listed from worst to best)

1. LifeStyles Nuda Plus

2. LifeStyles Extra Strength with Nonoxynol-9

3. LifeStyles Nuda

4. Mentor

5. Ramses NuForm

6. Pleaser Ribbed Lubricated (same as Saxon Ribbed Lubricated)

7. Ramses Sensitol Lubricated

8. Sheik Non-Lubricated Plain End

25 THINGS NOT TO SAY
IF YOU WANT TO KEEP YOUR LOVER*

1. "And I paid 15 cents for the parsley, so that means you owe me 7 ½ cents, but we can deduct it from the 23 ⅓ cents I owe you for soap, and that leaves..."

Two can live as cheaply as two, but if you count every last penny, you'll find that two can argue as well as four. Nothing comes out exactly even — not the expenses and not the amount you love each other. Settle for a general approximation.

2. "Isn't that my underwear you're wearing? No? Then where is mine?"

What could be more loving than sharing your Jockeys? But if one does all the wearing and shredding, and the other does all

---

* This list was supplied by Arnie Kantrowitz and previously appeared in *The Advocate*.

the buying and washing, you'll be sharing the suspicion and recriminations. Who wants to resent underwear? It could ruin a perfectly good fetish. On the other hand, who wants to pay for a tie he's going to wear only once? Decide at the beginning how to deal with sharing, and stick to your bargain. Separate rules for underwear and ties are permissible. If he can't understand why, show him this.

3. "Thanks for the athlete's foot (or flu, etc.)."
Be considerate. Sharing a fungus may be an opportunity to grow together, but the couple that itches together bitches together. If you've got something you don't want to share, shower without a friend. And when it comes to communicable diseases, safe sex might be an interesting variant on that intimacy you're starting to take for granted.

4. "Your mother called ... and kept me on the phone for half an hour — not that I don't enjoy an interesting discussion about bird watching now and again."
Save your sarcasm for public officials. You know how attached gay men are to their mothers, so don't come between hubby and his "best girl." If you don't want to talk about birds, make up a polite excuse. But if you do chat about the chickadees, it's your own responsibility.

5. "You mean you wrapped the garbage in the porn magazine? I was still reading it! Where are your brains?"
In the garbage with the magazine if you're not sensitive to what he cares about. Sometimes you may make an honest mistake. The proper response in that case is not a counterattack ("Take out your own garbage the next time, you pig!") but an apology ("I'll try to ask if you're finished next time. But why do you need a picture of that hunk when you've got me?"). Be careful with that last line, however; it could open another can of worms.

6. "I'm in the mood for ... oh, is it a bad headache?"
This moment eventually arrives even in the hottest of relationships. If it happens sixteen times in a row, suggest a good doctor.

If it happens once in a while, live with it, and save up your spunk for a hotter time tomorrow. If it never happens, drop dead.

7. "I'm in the mood for ... someone else."

Not until the epidemic is over. In the best of times, a little freedom could be a healthy change. And it always was tacky soap-opera behavior to check his collars for lipstick ... or his shorts for alien cum stains. These days, however, monogamy is survival. Without careful adherence to safe sex rules, variety is the spice of death. Enough said.

8. "This bed isn't big enough for both of us."

Somebody's hogging the blanket, and it isn't you. You'd think a queen-size bed could fit two queens. Don't just lie there listening him snore and cursing his unconscious form. Buy a bigger blanket or a bigger bed. Or cuddle up a little closer and remember what it felt like to cruise the streets at 4 a.m. in February. Ain't love grand?

9. "What do you mean I forgot to: (a) take out the garbage, (b) wash the dishes, (c) walk the dog?"

Make a reasonable arrangement, and keep up your share. If it's not working, try something else. Trade chores until you're happy, although you'll each probably have preferences. If you can't stand an unmade bed, make it yourself — as long as he empties his own ashtrays. If you both enjoy the "lived-in" look, fine. One warning: *Somebody'd* better walk the dog, or he'll burst his bladder on your new rug.

10. "I could stick to my diet if you didn't keep buying cookies and leaving them where I can find them."

You could stick to your diet if you didn't eat cookies period. Marriage is fattening, and it doesn't help if temptations are lying around begging to be consumed, but keeping in shape is your own responsibility. If he can eat cookies and stay thin, hate him, but don't blame him for your problems. Another possibility is to marry someone your own size. (Just make sure you buy a sturdy bed.)

11. "Sure, tell me all about it. (What do you care if I never get to sleep?)"

If you listen to his problems, he'll listen to yours, tit for tat. If you've listened, and he doesn't, there's trouble in paradise. The plain truth is you've got to be friends as well as lovers, or it's not a marriage: It's an extended trick. Listen, both of you. Marriage is not a picnic without ants.

12. "Your dick is smaller than mine. So there."

Somebody's dick has got to be smaller, but saying so is out of bounds. Besides, it really doesn't matter, or you wouldn't be together in the first place. Fight like gentlemen. Break dishes.

13. "Yes, dear."

Somebody's not listening. See number 11.

14. "Must you turn those pages so loudly?"

You're mad about something else. What is it? Most fights are about the wrong thing. Try not to waste time on trivia. Go for the jugular.

15. "I've never seen anyone eat cold pizza for breakfast."

You have now. If his mother couldn't change him, you can't either. You could plant nutrition pamphlets around the kitchen, but that's a form of armed aggression. Let him eat his own way. If you can't lick him, why are you married? Sorry. If you can't lick him, try joining him. Cold pizza can be quite delicious at dawn. Cold quiche, however, is another story. You do want a real man, don't you?

16. "Of course I'd like to listen to the *Ring* cycle again, dear."

Only if he'll agree to watch *All About Eve* for the 12th time. After negotiations, you may have to do without both, in which case your neighbors will probably thank you.

17. "My friends (family) are better than yours."

Don't be ridiculous. They're all awful.

18. "What do you mean those flowers are dead? They'll look good for another three days."

Yes, dear. (Ignore number 13.) Three days of looking at dead weeds isn't too high a price for keeping the peace.

19. "Why does your alarm clock have to wake me up an hour before I have to get up?"

Are you sure you don't mean, "Why do you have to go to sleep earlier than I do?" Try going to sleep together and waking up together. An extra hour in the morning could prove to be a treasure. If you don't take my advice, buy ear plugs, and I hope you sleep through your own alarm, you creep.

20. "It's a lovely picture, dear. (Why don't we hang it in the closet?)"

If he puts up with your Aunt Grace's marble platypus lamp, you can put up with his picture. Being gay men, you are, of course, afflicted with both extreme good taste and hypersensitivity; but being married, you'd better be gifted with some willingness to compromise. Look at it this way, at least your home won't have that phony decorated look. (You do *what* for a living? Oh, sorry. If you're a professional interior designer, tell him to hang the picture in the closet, and tell Aunt Grace not to drop in without calling, so you can get her lamp out of storage.)

21. "Why must you always be late (or so unfashionably prompt)?"

Poor upbringing in both cases. Learn to live with each other's habits, or learn to live without each other.

22. "*Your* dog just peed on *my* rug."

Our dog, our rug and our pee, or no dice. (See warning in number 9.)

23. "How many times do I have to tell you not to leave your clothes draped over the lamp? I'm not your maid."

See number 21. (You could call his mom to commiserate, but before you do, see number 4, on the joys of discussing bird watching.)

24. "Oh, your sister and her three kids are staying over for a week, and we won't be able to have sex? Terrific."

Hello, Aunt Grace? How'd you like to spend your vacation in our living room?

25. "Why do your clothes have to take up more than half the closet? Throw out that tacky (a) leather jump suit, (b) set of primary-color sports jackets, (c) ivory-lace bride's drag!"

Gay people seem to have endless problems with their closets. Put up a divider and stick to your own side. Better yet, empty all the closets and live free (if sparsely dressed).

Waltzing the Straight and Narrow

8 PROPOSED CAUSES OF HOMOSEXUALITY

1. THE PLANETS

Babylonian astrologers thought that Scorpio governed "love of a man for a man." Ptolemy, on the other hand, explained that, "joined with Mercury, in honorable position, Venus restrains some men in their affairs of love with women, but makes them more passionate for boys, and jealous."

2. PARENTAL ERROR

In the Hippocratic school of physicians, both parents were thought to secrete male or female "bodies." If the father's secretions were female, rather than male, and the mother's were male, the child would be either an effeminate male or a "mannish" female.

3. FAULTY PLUMBING

Aristotle believed that in "passive" homosexuals, the channels carrying sperm within the body were connected to the rectum instead of to the penis; in homosexuals who took both active and passive roles, the sperm flowed to both.

4. ITCHINESS

An Arab quoted in the West as late as the thirteenth century hypothesized that homosexual desires were caused by "excessive itchiness in the buttock region," and could be relieved by applying a salve to the area.

5. A SLUGGISH SPIRIT

In India, the doctrine of reincarnation has led some authorities to suggest that homosexuality results when a person changes gender from one life to the next: Though the physical body is easily changed during reincarnation, deeply ingrained "habits" such as sexual orientation may be slower to change.

6. NEGLECTED COLONS

In his book *Colon Health: The Key to a Vibrant Life,* Dr. Norman W. Walker writes:

As a matter of fact, when a woman is in as nearly a perfect health condition as is possible for her to be in this day and generation, she finds her intuitive faculties quite keen and alert. On the other hand, when the colon has been neglected for a lifetime, better instincts are dimmed and the mind leans toward self-pity, which often leads to such perversions as lesbianism. This is particularly the case when the tonsils have been removed.

7. THOUGHTFUL GENES
The relatively new science of sociobiology tries to explain homosexuality in terms of its contribution to the survival of the species. One hypothesis, based on the concept of *kin selection,* posits that homosexuality advances a species by freeing individuals from the reproductive cycle, so they can care for siblings, nieces, and nephews.

8. PORK CHOPS
According to Tasleed Amhed, a contemporary Islamic eye surgeon in Ireland, "It has been proven that the pig is the only homosexual animal. As this perversion [homosexuality] is most prevalent in pork-eating nations, it is obvious that it gets into your genes through your mouth."

7 DISTINCT TRAITS IN THE HANDWRITING OF GAY PEOPLE*

1. ORNATE CAPITAL LETTERS

2. SOFT, BALLOONING LETTERS

3. INCURVED CIRCLES

---

* These traits were reported by graphologist Eldene Whiting at the 1975 convention of the American Handwriting Analysis Foundation at the University of Santa Clara.

4. EXCESSIVE PUNCTUATION, SUCH AS DASHES, PAREN-
THESES, AND UNDERLINES

5. SUNKEN HUMPS ON THE LETTER "M"

6. T-BARS AND I-DOTS TO THE LEFT

7. A VARIED SLANT, REFLECTING AN AMBIVALENCE ABOUT
MALE–FEMALE IDENTITY

15 CASES OF CENSORSHIP WHERE NO SEX WAS INVOLVED

1. *KINGS ROW*
The 1941 movie based on this male-bonding novel by Henry
Bellamann omitted one subplot: a near-seduction of the
protagonist and his best friend by a pretty, but tortured pal.

2. PACIFIC BELL
In 1968, the Pacific Telephone and Telegraph refused to run
a display ad for the Society for Individual Rights in its yellow
pages. PT&T reversed itself only after the SIR took the matter to
the California Supreme Court in 1971.

3. MOUNTAIN BELL
In 1972, Mountain Bell Telephone Co. refused to list the Rev.
Carl Schmidt's Homosexual Church of the Universe under its
proper name. Instead, the listing in the Denver phone book read,
"Homophile Association of the Universe." Even the use of the
word *homophile* was a first, and was achieved only through
repeated efforts by the American Civil Liberties Union.

4. LEONARDO da VINCI
When CBS aired an Italian-made series on Leonardo da Vinci
in the U.S. in 1972, da Vinci's homosexuality had been obscured.
English had been dubbed in in place of the original Italian for the

U.S. broadcast, and a mistranslation in the pivotal scene made da Vinci appear to have been a heretic, rather than a homosexual. Whether the change was accidental or deliberate was never determined.

5. HOLLYWOOD PUBLIC LIBRARY
Not until July 1974 were books on homosexuality shelved in the open stacks at the Hollywood Public Library. Until then anyone who wanted a book on homosexuality had to first explain to the reference librarian why they wanted it.

6. GENNADY TRIFONOV
A Russian gay poet, he was sentenced to hard labor in the Soviet Union from 1976 to 1980 for privately circulating his poems. Since 1986 the Soviet government has allowed him to publish essays and reviews as long as he doesn't mention any gay topics.

7. "JAMESTOWN'S OTHER PEOPLE"
An exhibit honoring early settlers of the first permanent English settlement in North America was installed in Jamestown, Virginia, in 1980. It recognized the contributions of many groups, including the elderly, the handicapped, Native Americans, and gay people. In 1981, newly installed park superintendent Richard Maeder removed the plaque honoring gay people, bowing to letters of protest and an article in the *National Enquirer*.

8. "DECK THE HALLS"
A "Cabbage Patch Kids" float in the 1986 Macy's Thanksgiving Day Parade played the traditional Christmas carol with one small change to its lyrics: "Don we now our *fine* apparel/Fa la la la la..."

9. "THE LAMBDA REPORT"
The mayor of Warren, Michigan, a suburb of Detroit, and the third largest city in the state, refused in 1986 to allow "The Lambda Report," a gay cable news and feature program, on a public access channel in Warren. Though he had not seen the show, he "didn't think it was an appropriate subject for cable

television viewers." The half-hour show had already been shown in twenty-five other cities across the state.

10. *SEATTLE TIMES*

For many years, many daily newspapers (including the *Washington Post* and the *Los Angeles Times*) refused to run ads that contained the word *homosexual*. Some have altered that policy only slightly. In 1987, the *Seattle Times* barred the local Parents and Friends of Lesbians and Gays (PFLAG) from publishing a meeting announcement unless it changed the "Lesbians and Gays" in their name to "Homosexuals."

11. DALLAS CITIZENS WHO WANTED TO BE OUT

In 1988, three Dallas newspapers rejected a Coming Out Day advertisement. The ad listed the names or initials of 450 local gay men and lesbians who wanted to come out in the paper in celebration of the day. Why the rejection? The papers were afraid of being sued for libel by anyone with a name similar to one in the ad. The *Dallas Morning News* finally ran the ad two weeks later — but with all 450 names blacked out. An inset explained the reason for the censorship, pointing out the strong fear that still prevailed of the consequences of being identified as homosexual.

12. *WISCONSIN TROOPER*

A gay bar tried to run an ad in *Wisconsin Trooper,* published by the Wisconsin State Troopers Association, in 1988. Rejecting the original ad because it included the phrase *gay owned and operated,* the magazine accepted a revised ad that read instead, "non-heterosexually owned."

13. *MEN IN LOVE*

In 1989, police on the Hawaiian island of Maui recommended that no one under eighteen be allowed to see this film about a gay man whose lover dies of AIDS-related complications, even though the film contains no nudity or explicit sex.

14. HOLOCAUST EXHIBIT

In early 1990, the Salt Lake City school board removed an article about the Nazi persecution of gays from an educational exhibit about the Holocaust. It cited a Utah law that prohibits the teaching of "acceptance or advocacy of homosexuality as a desirable or acceptable sexual adjustment or lifestyle" in Utah schools. Opposition from gay, human rights, and religious groups finally forced the board to restore the article to the exhibit.

15. *GREEN BAY PRESS-GAZETTE*

Wisconsin's *Green Bay Press-Gazette,* a Gannett paper, turned down ads in 1990 for "gay–lesbian resources" and "hand-painted sweatshirts for lesbians."

6 WITCH-HUNTS

1. NEWPORT, RHODE ISLAND, 1919–1920

In 1919, officers at the Newport Naval Training Station sent several young enlisted men into the community to seek out "sexual perverts," have sex with them, and find out all they could about homosexual activity in Newport. Acting on the information these "decoys" obtained, authorities arrested more than twenty sailors and sixteen civilians.

Despite the number of people involved (and the investigation had reportedly been curtailed because so many were found to have engaged in homosexual activity!), their trials proceeded without controversy until a prominent clergyman was arrested — whereupon the Newport Ministerial Union and a local Episcopal bishop challenged the methods the Navy had used in its investigations. They subsequently persuaded the Senate Naval Affairs Committee to conduct its own investigation, and the committee ended up condemning the conduct of the officials involved.

2. BOISE, IDAHO, 1955–1956

The 1955 arrest of three men for having "seduced two young boys" — actually teenage hustlers — led to a wave of arrests and, fueled by inflammatory newspaper coverage, near-hysteria in the city of Boise. The hysteria peaked when *Time* magazine reported the uncovering of "a widespread homosexual underworld that involved some of Boise's most prominent men and has preyed on hundreds of teen-age boys for the past decade." Police imposed a curfew on youths under seventeen, all-male poker games and other gatherings were discontinued, and even watching high school football practice became suspect. In the end a dozen people were arrested — most of whom were guilty only of relations between consenting adults, despite all of the press about corruption of "our youth."

Ten years later, an investigation by journalist John Gerassi revealed that the whole affair had been a carefully orchestrated attempt by a conservative political clique to unseat a wealthy, powerful, closeted homosexual. Ironically, however, the man was so powerful that, though the police did, in fact, "have a talk" with him, his name was never mentioned in connection with the scandal, nor was he ever charged.

3. NORTHAMPTON, MASSACHUSETTS, 1960

In a local crackdown on pornography, seven Northampton men, including a nationally acclaimed literary critic and English professor, were arrested for possessing homoerotic books and pictures. Pressing the men for the names of others they had shown the materials to, the police claimed to have evidence of a multi-state "pornographic photo ring"; rumors of the "widening police net" caused high anxiety among gays throughout the area. No other arrests were made. All seven were found guilty and given suspended sentences; two were acquitted on appeal.

4. OFFUTT AIR FORCE BASE, OMAHA, NEBRASKA, 1970

An investigation that began with one Air Force sergeant became a witch-hunt that affected members of all the military services, civilian government employees, and residents of areas where U.S. military bases were located.

Under the threat of criminal prosecution and with the promise of being able to stay in the Air Force, Staff Sergeant Richard G. Burchill provided the names of some thirty men who he knew had engaged in homosexual practices. These in turn yielded other names. In the end investigators ended up with 270 names, including nicknames and first or last names only, and managed to fully identify 55 military personnel and 76 civilians. Sixteen airmen were immediately discharged, as was Burchill.

5. U.S.S. *NORTON SOUND,* LONG BEACH, CALIFORNIA, 1980

The Navy investigated sixteen out of sixty-one female crew members on the U.S.S. *Norton Sound* after an anonymous accusation that they had participated in "homosexual acts." In its investigation, the Navy repeatedly pressured one close friend of the accused women to make statements against them, transferring her off the ship as soon as she did so. The investigators also reportedly used strong-arm tactics and deception to force the accused to confess or "rat" on others. Eight women were ultimately charged; two were found not guilty, two guilty, and charges against the remaining four were dropped.

6. VINCENNES, INDIANA, 1986–1987

When eighteen-year-old Brent Brand passed out after a party and wouldn't wake up, the man who was with him, Jim Leyendecker, panicked, drove to a nearby town, and dumped his body in a ditch. The body was found there eight days later.

Brand's mother became convinced that he had been a victim of a "gay murder cult." Despite the failure of three autopsies and a police investigation to find any evidence of murder, the county prosecutor called for a grand jury inquiry, fueling anti-gay rumors by claiming — but later denying — that he was "investigating satanic, ritual homosexual practices." Other gossip maintained that the party Brand had attended was "an annual gathering" of prominent, closeted men, who killed Brand to protect their reputations. The local *Daily News* further stoked rumors by quoting Brand's mother saying, "It was a planned party and Brent was the target," and calling Brand's death "sacrificial." Some forty people were questioned by the grand jury, and several gays lost their jobs or were otherwise harassed as a result of the investigation and rumors. In the end, only Leyendecker was charged — with failure to report a death and moving a body without permission.

18 APOLOGIES FOR ANTI-GAY CONDUCT

1. MARTIN LUTHER KING III

Martin Luther King III, son of the civil rights leader, commented to a student group in Poughkeepsie, N.Y., in 1990 that "something may be wrong in the make-up of gays. Any man with a desire to be with another man has a problem, in my opinion. And that applies to any woman who has a desire to be with another woman."

After gay activists met with King, he publicly said that his remarks "were uninformed and insensitive ... I extend my sincere apologies to the entire community and, in particular, to the gay and lesbian community."

2. CHRISTINA ORR-CAHALL

As director of the Washington, D.C., Corcoran Gallery of Art, Christina Orr-Cahall cancelled an exhibit of photographs by Robert Mapplethorpe in 1989. Her effort to avoid controversy over the artwork, which included explicit depictions of gay sex and S&M, instead drew a storm of protests from artists and gay activists. She and the gallery's trustees apologized for the cancellation, and a few months later Orr-Cahall resigned.

3. PAT GARRETT

In 1989, Garrett, a disc jockey in Sacramento, was dumped by his girlfriend for a man named Bruce. In retaliation, Garrett commented on the air that all men named Bruce are "limp-wristed queers."

The city's human rights commission received several hundred complaints, and Garrett publicly apologized.

Congressman Barney Frank of Massachusetts has been openly gay since 1987.

4. Rep. CHUCK DOUGLAS

Conservative first-term congressman Chuck Douglas, who sat on the House Judiciary Committee with Barney Frank, remarked to committee members in 1989 that "I don't know if you know who Barney Frank is, but he's one of the two members there who are only interested in members of their own sex. That gives you a little feel for the [judiciary] committee."

After Frank remarked on this "mean-spirited performance," Douglas apologized by telephone, and a spokesman for Douglas said that "Chuck said this will not happen again."

5. A BILLBOARD OWNER

The owner of an electronic billboard in the Washington, D.C., financial district apologized and donated $5,000 to both an AIDS counseling center and a drug-abuse clinic after an employee repeatedly flashed the message "HELP STAMP OUT AIDS NOW: KILL ALL QUEERS AND JUNKIES!" He also fired the employee who had written the message.

6. KENNETH GLASSMAN

At a 1989 retirement roast for two police officers, Miami Beach police chief Kenneth Glassman joked that the two officers would probably make a lot of money "printing photos of missing gays on Vaseline jars." Apologizing later, he said he would dock himself two days' pay for the remark.

7. Judge JACK HAMPTON

Dallas judge Jack Hampton gave a light sentence to a convicted gaybasher and killer in 1988 with the remark that "these two guys that got killed wouldn't have been killed if they hadn't been cruising the streets, picking up teenage boys. I don't much care for queers cruising the streets, picking up teenage boys. I've got a teenage boy." He would have given the killer a stiffer sentence, the judge said, had the victims been "a couple of housewives out shopping." The comment drew angry criticism from church and civil rights leaders and public officials, and a month later Hampton apologized for "a poor choice of words."

8. STROH BREWERY CO.

As head of the advertising agency used by Stroh, Michael Lesser commented to the *Wall Street Journal* in January 1988 that "beer imagery is so delicate that getting associated with homosexuals could be detrimental."

In response, gay activists in Chicago formed the Coalition Against Media/Marketing Prejudice (CAMMP) and went to Stroh to ask if that was how the company wished to be represented. A company official declared Lesser's comments to be "uncalled for," and said that "Stroh understands the affront the gay and lesbian community must feel as a result of Mr. Lesser's comments."

9. THE DINER and IN CAHOOTS, INC.

The Stonewall Human Rights Organization of Greater Cincinnati organized a boycott joined by twenty-one other civic and political organizations after The Diner and two restaurants owned by In Cahoots allegedly fired eleven gay waiters in 1987. Though the principal owner of the restaurant chain denied that the firings were discriminatory, he did apologize for "what has been regarded as harassment based on sexual orientation" and agreed to review the firings. Two waiters were hired back (nine had found other jobs or did not want to return), and the company adopted an explicit nondiscrimination policy.

10. BOYS MARKET SUPERMARKET

When in 1987 an employee of Boys Market, a California supermarket chain, said over a store loudspeaker, "Faggots, get out of the market and don't come back," the three men at whom the directive was aimed sued. As part of the settlement the chain formally apologized to the men, banned discrimination within the company based on sexual orientation, and published an ad announcing that "Boys welcomes and encourages the patronage of the gay and lesbian community."

11. BOB HOPE

Bob Hope joked on a Fourth of July cruise in New York Harbor in 1986 that "nobody knows if she [the Statue of Liberty] got AIDS from the mouth of the Hudson or the Staten Island Ferry." After Wayne Friday of *The Bay Area Reporter* reported the incident, Hope apologized in a letter, saying, "I agree with you: the joke was uncaring and unnecessary. I told it and I apologize for it.... I am well aware, Wayne, that AIDS is no laughing matter and I shall continue to be part of the campaign in the fight against this dread disease." He later donated his time to a pro-gay, public service ad campaign.

12. MILLER BREWING CO.

During a speech at a 1983 banquet in Colorado that he was attending as a representative of the Miller Brewing Co., Frank Robinson, the field manager of the San Francisco Giants, said, "We've decided to go after the gay community this year. We're going to have a special section for them to sit. Instead of the grandstand, we're going to call it the fruit stand." The Miller company apologized in a letter to *The Advocate,* saying, "We consider Mr. Robinson's remarks about gay Americans to be offensive and improper. They do not, in any way, represent the feelings of the Miller Brewing Company."

13. *NEW YORK TIMES*

After the *Times* failed to cover a 1983 AIDS benefit by the Ringling Brothers Circus, the executive editor, A.M. Rosenthal, wrote to the gay community, "I really have no explanation for it [the lack of coverage] except for one of human error. It was an oversight and that's all I can say, except to express my regrets." Immediately afterward, the *Times* began running stories on the AIDS crisis almost every day, an action that attracted the attention of other major newspapers to the epidemic.

14. ED DALY

Ed Daly, then president of the cut-rate World Airways, wrote in a 1979 letter to employees, "The teamsters have gone on record in support of queers as reported recently in a San Francisco newspaper. This company doesn't need hoodlums, racketeers, queers." He retracted his statement the following year in a letter to the Golden Gate Business Association.

15. RICHARD PRYOR

During a 1977 gay rights benefit at the Hollywood Bowl, comedian Richard Pryor verbally assaulted his audience with such comments as "Give the money from this concert to the people on welfare," and "While the niggers in Watts were out there, you gays were up in Hollywood doing whatever you want to be doing. Kiss my black, rich ass!" Seven years later, he finally apologized, admitting, "I was drunk and I was doing some coke and I was an asshole and I hurt a lot of people and I apologize. I really don't mean those things."

16. CHARLIE BUSH and CHUCK KNAPP

In 1975, while working as radio announcers at station KSTP in St. Paul, Charlie Bush and Chuck Knapp joked about "gay blades," "fairy boats," and "fruit punch" after a news account about a change in Canada's policy toward gay immigrants. A Minneapolis attorney tried to get the station's management to apologize; when that failed, he filed a complaint with the FCC. Bush and Knapp ended up apologizing on the air after reading aloud the attorney's letter to the FCC.

17. Sen. JACOB JAVITS

While campaigning for re-election in 1974, Sen. Jacob Javits (R-NY) was asked his position on gay rights. Equivocating, he said he favored equality and justice for all individuals regardless of their sexual orientation, but quickly added that he personally found homosexuality "distasteful"; gays "don't know what they're missing," he quipped. He sent a formal, written apology to New York's gay community several weeks later, calling his comment an "unfortunate off-the-cuff remark."

18. JACK PAAR

Late night television host Jack Paar apologized on the air in 1973 for using the word "fairy" after Ronald Gold of New York's Gay Activists Alliance protested Paar's language. In a 45-minute telephone conversation with Gold, during which Paar revealed profound ignorance about homosexuality and the gay liberation movement, Paar also agreed to stop using language and telling jokes demeaning to gays, and to have GAA representatives appear on his show.

...AND 3 PEOPLE WHO HAVEN'T

1. Mayor JAMES GRIFFIN

Asked by the *Buffalo* (N.Y.) *News* in 1983 to comment on the planned move of a prominent gay bar to a larger site in Buffalo's theater district, the city's mayor said, "I'm against it and you can put that in the [expletive deleted] headlines. I don't use the term 'gay bars.' To me, they're not gays, they're fruits." Asked to apologize for his remarks by a gay rights group, Griffin again used the term fruit, along with "several other so-called derogatory characterizations of homosexuals" that the newspaper would not print.

2. ANDREW MARTIN

A millionaire insurance agent, Martin made frequent anti-gay statements while campaigning for a seat in the California state senate in 1984. Among the Democrat's jibes: "Those people like to call themselves 'gay,' but I don't consider them that. To me, the word is 'sad.'" And, "Those homosexual queers are good fund raisers — and by 'queer' I include lesbians." He said he often uses the word queer instead of gay or homosexual and makes no apology for doing so.

3. GIL FERGUSON
   A Republican assemblyman from Newport Beach, California, and a 1990 candidate for the state senate, Ferguson called a group of gay protesters "faggots." He said afterward, "I didn't even know that 'faggot' was a derogatory term ... that's what I've always heard them called. I know that people don't call them queers anymore. I won't call them gay, though. I don't think there's anything gay about it. It's depressing." The previous year, Ferguson had proposed a resolution at the Republican State Convention, calling on the party to ban clubs based on sexual orientation.

12 PEOPLE WHO VOLUNTARILY CAME OUT IN A VERY PUBLIC WAY, AND WHERE THEY DID IT

1. GERRY E. STUDDS, *U.S. congressman*
On the floor of the U.S. House of Representatives, 1983

2. HOWARD BROWN, *former New York City commissioner of health*
In a front-page interview in the *New York Times*, 1973

3. CRAIG CLAIBORNE, *chef*
In a cookbook

4. BARNEY FRANK, *U.S. congressman*
In a front-page interview in the *Boston Globe*, 1987

5. DAVID KOPAY, *former major-league football player*
In the *Washington Star*, 1975

6. MERLE MILLER, *writer*
In an essay for the *New York Times Magazine*

7. KARL HEINRICH ULRICHS, *lawyer*
In front of a convention of lawyers — in 1867

8. LEONARD MATLOVICH, *Air Force sergeant*
On the cover of *Time* magazine

9. DAVID LAYER, *American teenager*
In a *Newsweek* special issue about American teenagers, 1990

10. MARVIN LIEBMAN, *Conservative movement leader*
In *National Review*, 1990

11. KAREN BURSTEIN, *New York municipal judge*
By introducing her life-partner at her swearing-in ceremony as a new judge

12. MICHAEL LOWENTHAL, *class valedictorian at Dartmouth College*
At his commencement address, before 8,000 people, 1990

8½ PEOPLE WHO CLAIM TO HAVE BEEN "CURED" OF THEIR HOMOSEXUALITY

1. GLADYS BENTLEY
Notorious for her marriage to another woman, the black singer was miraculously cured of her lesbianism (and of "infantile" genitals) by hormone injections. She claimed falsely to be married to newspaper columnist J.T. Gibson, but later did marry a cook, Charles Robe?

2. DAVID CALIGIURI
This former gay man directs Free Indeed, a Phoenix organiza-

tion that offers "a way out of the homosexual death-style" through prayer.

3. GILES LAROCHE

Claiming to have been cured of his homosexuality by God, Laroche traveled across Vermont in 1986 carrying a fifty-pound cross in an effort to defeat the ERA in that state. Laroche was a member of Straight and Narrow, an organization that tries to convert gays to heterosexuality.

4. JAY WESLEY NEILL

Neill was convicted of killing four people during a 1984 holdup. Afterward, he declared in an interview on "The 700 Club," a fundamentalist Christian television program, that he had been "born again" as a Christian and "relieved" of his homosexuality. His death sentence has been stayed pending the outcome of automatic appeals.

5. ROBERT JACKSON

Jackson was the first firefighter in the country to be named liaison to a city's gay community. No longer: Jackson announced in 1988 that he had been born again and is no longer gay.

6. JONATHAN HUNTER

A former model and actor as well as a former homosexual, as of 1987 Hunter headed the AIDS Resource Ministry, a Los Angeles County organization that attempts, sometimes aggressively, to persuade homosexual PWAs to repent before they die and burn in hellfire.

7. ANDY COMISKEY

A self-described "former gay," Comiskey founded Desert Stream Ministries, one of the largest "ex-gay" Christian ministries in the U.S., and has served as president of Exodus International, a coalition of some fifty such ministries across the country. He also co-founded Homosexuals Anonymous, a fourteen-step program in which "the homosexual identity is replaced by the goal of realizing our new identity in Christ."

8. JOANNE HIGHLEY

Highley hid her lesbianism for ten years, even while performing as a gospel singer in evangelical churches. Now she and her husband, Ron Highley, head a New York ministry called LIFE (Living in Freedom Eternally), trying to help people break the addiction of homosexuality.

...and ½. COLIN COOK

Cook, a founder of Homosexuals Anonymous and the founder and director of the Quest Learning Center in Pennsylvania, which attempts to counsel gay people into becoming heterosexual, resigned in 1987 after fourteen men and boys seeking counseling at the center claimed he tried to have sex with them.

22 PEOPLE WHO CONFRONTED THE MILITARY

1. SERGEANT JOHNNIE PHELPS

When asked during World War II by her commanding officer, General Dwight Eisenhower, to ferret out the lesbians in her WAC battalion, Sergeant Phelps answered, "Sir, I'll be happy to do this investigation for you but you'll have to know that the first name on the list will be mine.... I think the General should be aware that among those women are the most highly decorated women in the war. There have been no cases of illegal pregnancies, ... no cases of AWOL, ... no cases of misconduct, and as a matter of fact, every six months the General has awarded us a commendation for meritorious service." Eisenhower replied, "Forget the order."

2. ROBERT A. MARTIN

Martin, a bisexual sailor who received a promotion while waiting for his case to be decided, was given a general discharge from the Navy in 1972 for being "unfit for military service." The discharge board's decision was unanimous, even though the

Navy's key witness repudiated statements he had made to Navy investigators. Martin appealed, but without success.

3. DEIDRE GREENE

Greene, a WAC stationed in San Antonio, Texas, made two trips to Washington in 1974 to declare herself a lesbian, thus challenging the Army's anti-homosexual policy. The Army sidestepped the challenge — probably because her term of duty was about to expire anyway — and responded merely by charging her with minor offenses, such as poor personal appearance.

4. JAMES WOODWARD

In 1972, when Woodward entered a Navy training program, he was perfectly honest about his attraction to men. The Navy accepted him nonetheless. But two years later he was removed from active service after being seen in the company of a sailor who was believed to be gay. Woodward challenged the dismissal. An appeals court decided in the Navy's favor, and in 1990 the U.S. Supreme Court refused to hear Woodward's case at the same time that it refused to hear that of Miriam ben-Shalom.

5. RUDOLF S. (SKIP) KEITH

A staff sergeant in the Air Force, Keith came out in 1975 during a race relations seminar, then spoke at New York City's Gay Pride rally with Leonard Matlovich and WACs Barbara Randolph and Debbie Watson. Keith was honorably discharged — in part because the action against him was only for homosexual "tendencies" and not for engaging in sexual activity while in the service. He tried, without success, to appeal the discharge.

6 & 7. BARBARA RANDOLPH and DEBBIE WATSON

Randolph and Watson were handed general discharges from the Army in 1975. The lovers, who worked for the Army Security Agency and belonged to an honor platoon, had voluntarily disclosed their relationship in response to increased harassment of gays under a new commanding officer. Because of their service records — Randolph had just been honored as WAC of the Month and Soldier of the Month and received an accelerated promotion — the two had hoped to simply be transferred into the regular army.

8. GARY NEWTON HESS

While a commander in the Naval Reserve, Hess sat on a panel discussing homosexuality and implied that he himself was gay. Another officer saw him and reported it to a superior. Hess was discharged; he sought to file suit, but without success.

9. VERNON E. BERG III

A Navy ensign, Berg was a member of the personal staff of the admiral of the Sixth Fleet in 1975. There, he handled top secret communications; his security clearance was in fact upgraded from "secret" to "top secret" during the investigation of his homosexuality. Though he initially resigned from the service when told of the investigation, he later retracted the resignation to fight his case.

He was given a dishonorable discharge, which was upgraded on appeal to honorable. He appealed further, seeking re-enlistment, but when Ronald Reagan assumed the presidency, Berg and his attorneys made a tactical decision to end his appeals and accept a cash settlement from the Navy. Berg agreed not to re-enlist, "which by that time," he says, "was just fine with me."

10. DENNIS BELLER

Beller was discharged from the Navy in 1976, despite an excellent service record. His case was taken as far as the Supreme Court, which declined his appeal.

11. PATRICIA VELDON

A review board attempted to discharge Veldon from the Navy for having "homosexual tendencies" following an alleged affair between her and an Air Force woman. Veldon appealed, and in a move that surprised most observers, the Bureau of Naval Personnel overturned the ruling, in part for lack of proof, in part because the Secretary of the Navy had recently ruled that the Navy was not required to discharge all homosexual personnel.

12. MIRIAN BEN-SHALOM

Ben-Shalom's lengthy clash with the military began in 1976, when, as a member of the Army reserves, she came out in a military newspaper. The case was decided in her favor by several courts, and she was the first openly gay person ever reinstated by the military. But the Army repeatedly appealed; in 1989 an appeals court ruled against her, and the U.S. Supreme Court in 1990 refused to hear a further appeal. This left ben-Shalom with no further recourse, though it set no binding precedent for future court decisions elsewhere in the country.

13. DIANE MATTHEWS

Ousted from ROTC in 1981 for declaring that she was a lesbian, Matthews initially won reinstatement in a federal court, but an appeals panel later ordered the lower court to reconsider. After the U.S. Supreme Court's ruling in June 1986 that private, consensual gay sex is not protected under the Constitution, Matthews, who won her initial suit on First Amendment grounds, decided to drop her fight.

14. JAMES DRONENBURG

Discharged from the Navy in 1981 for acknowledging that he engaged in homosexual acts, Dronenburg sued for reinstatement and lost. An appeals panel upheld the ruling and later denied Dronenburg's request for a rehearing by the full circuit.

15. MEL DAHL

After the Navy discharged him in 1982 for being gay, Dahl filed suit in a Chicago federal court. To raise funds and gain publicity, Dahl completed a seven-month-long cross-country march from the Statue of Liberty to San Francisco.

16. DAVID MARIER

An aircraft commander, Marier was discharged from the Air Force in 1985 after a fellow gay man informed on him and five others. Three of the others agreed to identify further homosexuals and were given discharges that were termed "honorable."

Marier's discharge, because he refused to finger others, was termed "other than honorable."

17. ELLEN NESBITT

Nesbitt's homosexuality was discovered during an investigation initiated by the Air National Guard to upgrade her security clearance to "top secret." Though offered an honorable discharge if she would leave voluntarily, she instead chose to fight her discharge.

18. BARBARA BAUM

In 1988, the Marine Corps charged twelve women at its Parris Island, S.C., base with lesbian activity. Baum was one of them. A court-martial panel convicted her and she spent eight months in prison. The conviction was overturned the next year by the Court of Military Review when several irregularities came to light, including the fact that one juror had openly expressed bias against lesbians. Baum is now suing the military for the $14,000 in costs she incurred during the trail.

19. RICARDO HUERTAS

As a chief petty officer with the Coast Guard, Huertas found that after eleven years of service, "my feelings toward men were getting stronger." He told his superior officer that he was gay, and requested shore duty. Ten shipmates testified on his behalf, but to no avail, and Huertas was discharged.

20. PERRY WATKINS

Watkins was denied re-enlistment after fourteen years, even though his superior officers had long known he was gay. In a precedent-setting decision, a U.S. appeals court ruled in 1988 that homosexuals are entitled to the same civil rights protection as racial minorities and ordered the Army to reconsider his application for re-enlistment. The Army has appealed, however, and the Supreme Court has agreed to review the case.

21. JOSEPH STEFFAN

As a midshipman at the U.S. Naval Academy, Steffan was one

day asked if he was gay. Rather than lie, he answered affirmatively. And so, four weeks before he would have graduated, Steffan was forced to resign. With support from the Lambda Legal Defense and Education Fund, he filed suit against the Navy in December of 1988.

A year later, a U.S. district court refused the Navy's first motion to dismiss, which was a partial victory for Steffan. However, when the Navy questioned Steffan about his conduct, his attorney advised him not to answer, on the grounds that he was dismissed for *being* gay, not for *engaging* in homosexual acts, and so questions about conduct had no bearing on the case. The judge then granted a Navy request that the suit be dismissed because the plaintiff was uncooperative. Steffan is appealing that decision.

22. JAMES HOLOBAUGH

In 1988, James Holobaugh was such an ideal member of the ROTC program that the Army put him on a recruiting poster. But a year later, he had come to realize that he was gay. He confided in an officer; soon the military had thrown him out of the program and demanded he repay his $25,000 ROTC scholarship.

With support from the American Civil Liberties Union, Holobaugh challenged that demand. Congressional and public pressure forced the Army to back down in Holobaugh's case. However, ROTC officials are continuing to demand repayment from others who are not willing or able to get as much publicity for their cases.

10 COPS

1. RUDI COX

Although other police officers had been quietly open about their sexual orientation in the past, the country's first publicly gay law enforcement officer seems to have been Rudi Cox, a black man hired as a deputy in 1976 by San Francisco Sheriff Richard Hongisto.

The road there hadn't always been easy. Cox revealed that he and other recruits had been required to study anti-gay texts as part of their training at the Alameda (California) County Sheriff's Academy. Among other things, academy instructors had taught that homosexuals recruited teenagers and posed a threat to civilization.

2. STEVE HORN
Not every city has been as accepting as San Francisco. Steve Horn of Mesa, Arizona, was dismissed as a narcotics officer in 1980 when he came out to Police Chief Joe Quigley. Horn, a four-year police veteran, was a model officer and had received a bronze star for heroism in Vietnam.

With the help of the ACLU, Horn engaged in a lengthy but unsuccessful legal battle. His case failed to overturn Arizona's sodomy statute, which had been cited as the reason for his dismissal.

3. DENISE KREPS
When Denise Kreps applied to become a deputy sheriff in Contra Costa County, near San Francisco, County Sheriff Richard Rainey refused to hire her because she was a lesbian. Kreps took the case to court and won; the judge ruled in 1980 that Rainey had failed to provide "any evidence other than speculative that showed that she couldn't do the job." Kreps was hired, and graduated at the top of her training class the following year.

4. PAUL SEIDLER
In 1980, when San Francisco mayor Dianne Feinstein resurrected several community relations positions within the city's police department, ten-year-veteran Paul Seidler came out and applied for the position of police liaison to the lesbian and gay community. He got it.

Among his fellow officers, Seidler teaches sensitivity to lesbian and gay issues. He also keeps the department abreast of concerns and developments within the community. He sees his main concern, however, as teaching lesbians and gay men that they can rely on the police.

5. CHARLES COCHRANE

Sergeant Charles Cochrane was once New York City's only openly gay officer, but no longer. In 1982 he founded GOAL (Gay Officers Action League); within two years, four other police officers and sixty civilian criminal-justice workers had joined the group.

6. ROBERT ALMSTEAD

The District of Columbia got its first openly gay police officer in 1981. Robert Almstead graduated first in marksmanship and third in his class overall at the police academy. As a rookie, his first partner was Bonnie Davenport — a transsexual who had served on the force both before and after her sex-change operation.

7. MITCH GROBESON

Police sergeant Mitch Grobeson's difficulties started in 1984, after a fellow officer stopped him outside a predominantly gay club in West Hollywood, then called a supervisor at the Los Angeles Police Department and told him that Grobeson was gay.

Four years of harassment followed, during which fellow precinct officers verbally abused him and even endangered his life by refusing to provide backup when he called for help. The campaign of hate finally drove Grobeson from the department.

8. MICHAEL FOLEY

Michael Foley joined the police force of Hazel Park, Michigan, in 1969, and in his words, "Not only have I not been in the closet, but I have made absolutely no effort to conceal my homosexuality."

Fifteen years later, when a friend was harassed by Detroit police, Foley protested and identified himself as a police officer. He was called a "faggot," and both he and his friend were arrested. They were cleared of all charges, and Foley countersued. In 1988, a federal jury awarded Sergeant Foley $65,000 in his lawsuit against the Detroit police.

9. AMBROSE SIMMS

As he became more comfortable with his own gayness, black Miami police officer Ambrose Sims became less comfortable with the confines of the closet. He came out in a 1989 letter to the *Miami Herald,* writing that his only alternative was "to live in a suffocating prison of cowardice." But instead of being fired or hounded from the force, as he had feared, Sims was told by his chief that "I would never fire you for being gay." Simms later started the Gay and Lesbian Police Officer Association.

10. TOM WOODARD

For five years, Woodard served on the police force in Orlando, Florida. In 1989, soon after he had been promoted to deputy sheriff, an internal affairs investigation revealed that Woodard was gay. Orange County Sheriff Walt Gallagher threatened to make the investigation public unless Woodard quietly resigned.

Woodard did, but the report was made public anyway. Woodard is now fighting in the courts to get his job back.

7 OPENLY GAY MEN AND LESBIANS WHO HAVE BEEN ORDAINED

1. WILLIAM JOHNSON, United Church of Christ, 1972.

Johnson was the first openly gay person to be ordained into a Christian ministry. The ordination took place in San Carlos, California, on the third anniversary of the Stonewall riots and the fifteenth anniversary of the U.C.C.

2. ELLEN MARIE BARRETT, Episcopal Church, 1977.

The first open lesbian to be ordained in a major religious denomination, Barrett was also among the first women to be ordained as priests in the Episcopal Church.

3. ROD REINHART, Episcopal Church, 1986.

Though the denomination's national convention had narrowly voted against ordaining open homosexuals, a dissenting bishop ordained Reinhart as a priest in 1986.

4. ROBERT WILLIAMS, Episcopal Church, 1989.

Simply by ordaining Williams, the liberal bishop John Spong raised the ire of many colleagues. But the outburst grew worse as Williams, out of either naivete or a hunger for the spotlight, commented at a church convention that Mother Teresa would be better off if she "got laid."

5–7. JEFF JOHNSON, PHYLLIS ZILLHART, and RUTH FROST, Evangelical Lutheran Church in America.

In 1990 the denomination suspended the two San Francisco congregations that ordained these three openly gay ministers, as well as suspending the three individuals. If the congregations do not revoke the ordinations, and the E.L.C.A.'s anti-gay policy does not change, in five years they will be expelled from the national church.

...AND 17 WHO HAVE COME OUT SINCE THEIR ORDINATION

1. TOM MAURER, United Church of Christ.

Maurer came out in 1969, twenty-six years after he was ordained, when he became director of a study on homosexuality for the Kinsey Institute. In 1973 his ordination was affirmed, after some resistance, by the U.C.C.'s association in Minneapolis.

2. GENE LEGGETT, United Methodist Church.

Leggett lost his ministerial credentials in 1971 when he came out as a homosexual. He was eventually hired as a janitor by a San Antonio church, where he also assisted in worship services and taught Sunday School classes; in 1975 the congregation voted to support him in his bid for restoration.

3. ROBERT HERRICK, Episcopal Church.

Herrick came out several years after he was ordained and left his church post to work for the National Gay Task Force in the mid-1970s.

4. RICHARD J. McAFFEE, Disciples of Christ Christian Church.

Ordained in 1973, three years later McAffee told the denominational publishing house where he worked that he was gay and planned to work privately for gay rights. They asked him to resign, and fired him when he refused.

Help came from an unexpected quarter: A small church in St. Louis offered him a ministry at their church, which, though predominantly heterosexual, was located at the periphery of the city's "gay ghetto." McAffee accepted, and began an active outreach program into the gay community.

5. JOHN McNEILL, Catholic Church.

After publication of his book, *The Church and the Homosexual,* in the 1970s, McNeill, an openly gay Jesuit priest and psychotherapist, was ordered by the Vatican to remain silent on the issue of homosexuality and sexual ethics. He did so for ten years, until the Church ordered him to stop all public ministry to gay people.

6. PAUL ABELS, United Methodist Church.

Controversy over Abels erupted in 1977 when the *New York Times* reported that the openly gay minister of Washington Square Church in New York City's Greenwich Village was performing "covenant ceremonies" for same-sex couples and was himself living with someone. Three years later, after much hoopla, the denomination's judicial council granted him permission to continue his ministry. Abels retired in 1984.

7. ALLEN B. BENNETT, Judaism.

The first rabbi to publicly acknowledge his homosexuality,

Bennett was appointed rabbi of a San Francisco synagogue in 1979.

8. ROBERT F. HUMMEL, Catholic Church.
Openly gay, Father Hummel was defrocked in 1979 for allegedly not remaining celibate.

9. RICHARD WAGNER, Catholic Church.
Wagner identified himself as gay, and wrote in the *National Catholic Reporter* in 1980 that the practice of celibacy by priests could lead to "severe psychological conflict." He further wrote that in a study of fifty homosexual priests, he had found that nearly all disagreed with the Church's position on homosexuality and celibacy, and that forty-eight had sex — on an average of twice a week. After Wagner refused to change his lifestyle or leave the priesthood, the Church dismissed him.

10. JULIAN RUSH, United Methodist Church.
Pressured to leave the ministry in 1981 after he came out to an unsympathetic colleague, Rush found support from Bishop Melvin E. Wheatley, Jr., who prevailed against all resistance to help Rush retain his credentials and secure a position at a church in a gay neighborhood of Denver. This was the first time an openly gay Methodist minister had been appointed to a pastoral position by a bishop. Despite persistent efforts to oust him from the church, the denomination's council repeatedly upheld Rush's right to minister, since it could not be shown that he was a "practicing" homosexual.

11. BRIAN SCOTT, Southern Baptist Church.
Believing that "homosexuality was caused by demon possession or at least a form of it," Scott went through an excorcism while in seminary. It didn't work, and six months after his ordination, Scott decided it was God's will that he remain gay. He went on to found a Gay–Lesbian Christian Fellowship in 1982; two years later the church that had ordained him revoked his ordination and terminated his membership. Scott continued his G.L.C.F. ministry nonetheless.

12. LINDA HOLTZMANN, Judaism.

Holtzmann, the first woman rabbi in the world to have her own pulpit in a Conservative Jewish synagogue, was also the first rabbi to be hired by Congregation Beth Ahavah, a gay synagogue in Philadelphia.

13. WILLIAM DORN, Jr., Catholic Church.

In 1986, Dorn wrote an article in a diocesan newspaper urging the Church to view homosexuality, like all sexuality, as a "blessing." He was summarily fired from his position as co-pastor at the Minnesota Newman Center. Three weeks later he came out to his parishioners, and the church stripped him of his priestly powers to perform the sacraments.

14. ROSE MARY DENHAM, United Methodist Church.

Though Denham had adamantly supported the 1984 UMC ruling to bar any "self-avowed, practicing homosexual" from being ordained, she soon discovered that she herself was gay. Taking a leave of absence, she later informed her bishop of her homosexuality; he eventually filed a complaint against her after she refused to leave the ministry. In the subsequent church trial, the jury found her "in violation" of church law, but handed down a sentence that allowed her to transfer her credentials to the Unitarian Universalist Association.

15. JIM JORGENSON, Catholic Church.

Jorgenson took an indefinite leave of absence from the Church in 1988 so that he could openly discuss his homosexuality and help dispel the image that the only gay clergy who come out of the closet are those who have AIDS or are accused of child molestation.

16. ANTONIO A. FELIZ, Church of Latter-Day Saints.

Feliz, a Mormon bishop who was excommunicated for divorcing his wife, described his coming out in his 1988 memoirs, *Out of the Bishop's Closet.*

17. MARGARITA SUAREZ, United Church of Christ.

As of 1990, Suarez was one of ten openly gay clergy members in the U.C.C. She is now pastor of a 200-member church in Milwaukee. Says Suarez about being out, "My faith tells me that all of me is a gift of God, and so I am going to share all of my God-given gifts with the community I serve."

17 STRAIGHT FRIENDS WE'RE GLAD TO HAVE

1. FERDINAND LASALLE
Even back in the late nineteenth century, Lasalle was advocating for gay rights in Germany.

2. MARGARET NEALL HAY
In 1951, the young Mattachine Society — precursor of the modern gay movement — formed a Mattachine Foundation to serve as an incorporated, nonprofit body that would provide legitimacy in dealing with the press and the public. The first president was Margaret Neall Hay, the mother of gay activist Harry Hay. Her name appeared in news stories, her address was on record in a homosexual context, and she opened the Mattachine bank account. Margaret Hay was politically conservative and did all of this simply out of support for her son; she never participated in Mattachine planning or political discussions.

3. HELEN KREISLER
Early in the 1970s, the elderly Kreisler became familiar with — and to — the gay community through a nephew who came out to her. She participated in gay pride marches carrying a sign that read "I'm not a drag, but I sure think these laws are!"

4. GEORGE WEINBERG
In 1972, Weinberg introduced the word and the concept *homophobia* with his book *Society and the Healthy Homosexual.*

5. SHIRLEY CHISHOLM

Chisholm, a former congresswoman from New York and the country's first black woman to seek a major party nomination for the presidency, was an early and outspoken supporter of civil rights for gay people.

6. AL GORDON

When his son was arrested for "lewd conduct," Los Angeles attorney Al Gordon first tried to convince himself that it had been a momentary lapse. But he felt a wall developing between him and his son and he sought counseling from the Rev. Troy Perry, head of the newly formed Metropolitan Community Church. Gordon quickly became a strong supporter of gay rights. He put his legal skills to use early in the 1970s, defending a number of important gay-rights cases.

7. NICK CARDAMONE

During a voter registration drive in Tucson, Nick Cardamone often went into gay bars and became acquainted with the discrimination that gay people face. He suggested that they organize, but to no avail. So in 1976 Cardamone — a political-science major who was also a member of the NAACP and a Chicano organization — started the Tucson Gay Coalition.

8. GEORGE BANDA

Banda, the owner of two gay clubs in San Francisco, became head of the gay Tavern Guild in 1981. Even then, he already had a long history of championing gay causes and helping with fundraising for them.

9. The Rev. JUNE NORRIS

In 1971, the 51-year-old mother became the first non-gay minister in the Metropolitan Community Church. In the years to come, she took part in sit-ins and marches on behalf of gay rights, in addition to her MCC work.

10. Dr. MATHILDE KRIM

Dr. Krim is best known to the gay community for her tireless

AIDS work, culminating in her co-founding of AmFAR (the American Foundation for AIDS Research). She is not new to activism, however: after surviving Nazi atrocities in World War II, she was a gunrunner for the new Israeli state. She then moved to the U.S. and was active in many political causes, including the NAACP.

11. MEG UMANS

As a librarian in the 1970s, Umans made sure that the Phoenix Public Library provided a good range of lesbian and gay materials. She later opened Humanspace Books in Phoenix, providing the city's best source of lesbian, gay, and feminist reading matter; and she is the editor of *Like Coming Home,* a collection of coming-out letters.

12. ADELE STARR

When he was eighteen, Adele Starr's son wrote her and her husband a short note: "I'm a homosexual. I cannot live here anymore. I will get in touch with you." He then banished himself from their home.

"I was in a great deal of despair," recalled his mother. But rather than give in to that despair, she co-founded a gay-positive group for parents in her situation. There are now similar groups in over a hundred cities.

13. BOB CARLSON

Chester's Used Books and Records, a bookstore run by Bob Carlson, is housed in a former movie theater. When a neighboring business put up an anti-gay sign in 1985, Carlson used his marquee for the message "AID GAYS: QUARANTINE BIGOTS."

14. CORETTA SCOTT KING

King, the widow of Dr. Martin Luther King, has publicly proclaimed her "solidarity with the gay and lesbian community," saying, "I believe all Americans who believe in freedom, tolerance, and human rights have a responsibility to oppose bigotry and prejudice based on sexual orientation."

15. DAVID BUNNELL

Instead of computer talk, lead editorials in the November 1986 issues of *PC World* and *MacWorld* magazines contained gay-rights commentary. Outraged at the Supreme Court's recent sodomy ruling, straight editor David Bunnell wrote that the "personal computer world should think twice about supporting high-tech development in states [such as Georgia] that lack a decent social climate for high-tech to operate in." About $32,000 in advertising was yanked by companies upset with Bunnell's editorials, but he made no apologies. "We can't let the fundamentalist right-wing Christians take over the country," he said.

16. The Rev. WILLIAM OLIVER

In the late 1980s, Rev. Oliver headed Citizens for a United Houston, a coalition of organizations working for gay rights in the city.

17. GLORIA ALLRED

This prominent attorney and feminist has long fought for gay rights. In 1982, when California state senator John Schmitz called her a "slick butch lawyeress," she sued and won $20,000. She donated the money to groups representing gays, Jews, and other minorities that were regularly defamed by the senator.

2 LOCALES THAT CHANGED THEIR NAMES...

1. GAY COURT, in La Verne, California

A year after the Stonewall Riots, residents of this quiet California street complained that the name had taken on a new meaning. The city council granted their request that the name be changed to Bayberry Court.

2. GAY MOUNTAIN of North Carolina

Ten years later, landowners on this mountain had the same complaint. It was renamed Misty Mountain.

...AND 14 THAT DIDN'T

1. FERRYSBURG, Michigan
   During the 1980s, residents tried several times to change the name of this town in western Michigan. "I'm just tired of the jokes every time I tell someone where I'm from," explained one resident. Nothing came of the attempts.

2. GAY, Kentucky
   A resident of this small Kentucky town petitioned the county for a name change in 1990. So far, nothing has come of the request.

3. GAYS, Illinois
   The old-timers feel fine about the name of this town of 300, but new residents sometimes are uncomfortable with it, says a town official. What they're really proud of is their two-story outhouse.

4. GAYVILLE, South Dakota
   No one here has shown any desire to see the town's name changed. Nor are the following names likely to come off the map any time soon:

5. DIKE, Texas

6. DYKE, Virginia

7. FORT GAY, Wyoming

8. FRUITLAND, Maryland

9. FRUITVALE, Idaho

10. GAY, Georgia

11. GAY, Michigan

12. GAYS CREEK, Kentucky

13. GAYS MILLS, Wisconsin

14. GAYSVILLE, Vermont

4 HINTS FROM THE LESBIAN CONNECTION ABOUT HOW STRAIGHT WOMEN SHOULD ACT WHEN THEY MEET A LESBIAN

1. DO NOT RUN SCREAMING FROM THE ROOM

2. DO NOT EXPECT HER TO BE AS EXCITED ABOUT MEETING A HETEROSEXUAL AS YOU MAY BE ABOUT MEETING A LESBIAN

3. DO NOT ASSUME SHE IS ATTRACTED TO YOU

4. DO NOT ASSUME YOU ARE NOT ATTRACTED TO HER

FROM WHENCE WE CAME

STUART TIMMONS'S
12 MOST IMPORTANT LESBIAN AND GAY
ACTIVISTS FROM ALL OF HISTORY*

Lesbian and gay rights simply would not exist without activists. They brave boring meetings, an often resistant constituency, and little recognition. All of them are important and every name here counts for at least ten more. With their courage, vision, and love, activists have truly changed the world.

1. SAPPHO
    A Greek citizen of the sixth century B.C., she achieved fame as a poet, a teacher, and a homosexual. Sappho was exiled from her home, the island of Lesbos, and later persecution destroyed all but fragments of her verses which describe the "delicate fire" of one woman's love for another. Nevertheless, her memory gives a name to all women-loving women.

2. KARL HEINRICH ULRICHS
    Born in 1825, the German lawyer wrote more than a dozen pamphlets advocating a liberation struggle for homosexuals, whom he called "Urnings." His campaign to decriminalize same-sex love even included public statements nearly one hundred years before Stonewall.

3. OSCAR WILDE
    He once visited America stating nothing to declare but his genius, and history agrees that the Irish essayist and playwright had a lasting impact on his culture. While never an activist, Wilde's notoriety from an 1895 trial about his love life put the term "homosexual" in newspapers and public conversation, thus beginning the gay century.

---

* Stuart Timmons is the author of *The Trouble with Harry Hay: Founder of the Modern Gay Movement*.

4. EDWARD CARPENTER

Scholarly, enlightened, and English, Carpenter trained at first for the clergy. In his many writings, he advocated economic reform, women's liberation, animal rights, and appreciation for practitioners of "homogenic love." Carpenter's ideas that homosexual people have distinct personality traits and necessary social roles are still revolutionary.

5. NATALIE BARNEY

Turn-of-the-century Paris, famous for its lesbians, had at its center the American Pullman car heiress, Natalie Barney. She openly declared her lesbianism in poetry and maintained a salon at her home which included novelists Djuna Barnes and Radclyffe Hall, painter Romaine Brooks, and poet Anna Wickham. Barney's aesthetic contributions to gay art and generous patronage of many gay artists spanned sixty years.

6. MAGNUS HIRSCHFELD

The "Hirschfeld Movement" galvanized his native Germany in the early twentieth century and was known throughout Europe. Originally a neurologist, Hirschfeld became a pioneering sexologist and interviewed thousands of "intermediates." He organized a committee of scientists to publicly campaign against sexually repressive laws, and created an institute of sexual research that was destroyed by the Nazis in 1933.

7. HARRY HAY

The radical scholar and organizer known as the Father of Gay Liberation at first dedicated himself to Marxism. Inspired by that vision and the statistics of Dr. Alfred Kinsey, Hay created the Mattachine Society, America's first gay organization. It spread nationwide, and established gays as a minority group. Hay's part in the spiritual Radical Faerie movement of the 1980s furthered his reputation as a seminal gay visionary.

8 & 9. DEL MARTIN and PHYLLIS LYON

Founders of the Daughters of Bilitis, the first American lesbian organization, this pair of lovers also published *The Ladder,* which bore light to untold thousands of women in the darkness of social invisibility. Authors of *Lesbian/Woman*, they remain together and active after four decades.

10. HARVEY MILK

An actor-turned-politician, Harvey Milk became a martyred gay activist. His theatrical style and powerful speaking ability saw him elected as San Francisco's first openly gay supervisor and as a nationwide spokesperson for gay rights. His assassination in 1978 by a homophobic political rival caused a major riot.

11 & 12. LARRY KRAMER and VITO RUSSO. Russo's *Celluloid Closet* exposed, with wit and charm, Hollywood hypocrisy. Kramer's novel *Faggots* and his play *The Normal Heart* did nothing but offend with their respective blasts at gay manners and AIDS policy. But the clashing manners of the two writers balanced perfectly in 1987 — they founded ACT UP, the AIDS Coalition to Unleash Power. Now that's making history!

11 PEOPLE FROM HISTORY AND LITERATURE THAT JOAN NESTLE WOULD MOST LIKE TO INVITE TO DINNER AT THE LESBIAN HERSTORY ARCHIVES*

1. MABEL HAMPTON (1902–1989), because she loved good company, good food and could talk up a storm. At the end of the meal, she would grace the table with her words and a twinkle, "Bless the Lord and Bless the cook, for these few mouthfuls I have took."

2. COLETTE (1873–1954), in her late years when her eyes glinted

---

* Joan Nestle is the co-founder and guiding light behind the Lesbian Herstory Archives, with which she shares an apartment in New York.

Emma Goldman, early feminist activist. Her favorite sexual activity was reportedly receiving cunnilingus — from either a man or a woman. Perhaps she could be responsible for dessert?

with her knowledge of the body, the knowledge both of pain and pleasure. I want to thank her for the kiss in *Vagabond*. Missy can come, too.

3. STEPHEN, created in 1928, star of *Well of Loneliness*. I hope she would wear her riding suit. She could bring Madame Bovary, who has a lot to offer.

4. MAY SWENSON (1919–1989), because Lee, my lover, showed me the wonders of her poems. May wrote about lean hard women with soft paws. We would compare notes.

5. LORENA HICKOCK (1893–1968), because she is the one with stories to tell about the girls. Mabel would have a ball getting the scoop: "Was *she* in the life?"

6. ZORA NEALE HURSTON (1903–1960), because she would outsass us all, because we need to thank her for Janie, because we lost her.

7. EMMA GOLDMAN (1869–1940), who would say the *Shabbas* prayer and include in it a plea for dancing and making love as part of the new order.

8 & 9. FEDERICO GARCIA LORCA (1898–1936) and LANGSTON HUGHES (1902–1967), because they would be a wonderful couple, full of passion and quiet. Perhaps Langston and Zora would make up.

10. KATHLEEN FERRIER (1912–1953), who died too young and sang so beautifully; her rendition of "Sapphishe Ode" is a gift to us. Perhaps she would sing "Buddy" with Mabel after dinner.

11. LORRAINE HANSBERRY (1930–1965), who needed a night out with the girls. We could argue about her letter to *The Ladder*.

I would help Lee, Lucinda, and Nancy prepare the dinner. Before eating, I would give all the guests a tour of the Lesbian Herstory Archives so they could see they had been to this home before.

THE 10 PEOPLE FROM THROUGHOUT HISTORY THAT PAT CALIFIA WOULD MOST LIKE TO INVITE TO A DINNER PARTY*

The Victorian era was full of contradictions. This period in history usually makes us think of vehement, comically misguided moral reformers. But alongside this sexual repression we can locate the origins of sex research, the flowering of the modern sex industry, and the development of urban subcultures for gay men, lesbians, and other sexual minorities. I've always wanted to host a dinner

---

* Pat Califia is a leading lesbian S/M activist. Her books include *Macho Sluts* and *Doc and Fluff*, and she writes the "Adviser" column in *The Advocate*.

party at which I could introduce some of the movers and shakers of Queen Victoria's reign to their modern counterparts.

1. HAVELOCK ELLIS
   First on my list is the author of *Studies in the Psychology of Sex,* a seminal work that Ellis published in several revised editions from 1896 to 1928. This was one of the first attempts to gain a cross-cultural perspective on human sexuality. Ellis examined sexual variation without viewing it as toxic. *Sexual Inversion,* his collaboration with John Addington Symonds, was one of the first English-language books to argue for increased acceptance of homosexuality, and was involved in a censorship case in 1898 that resulted in the book being withdrawn from circulation in England.

2. ALFRED KINSEY
   Who could I choose to sit next to Ellis other than Kinsey, the author (with others) of *Sexual Behavior in the Human Male* (1948) and *Sexual Behavior in the Human Female* (1953)? Kinsey, born in 1894, was himself a child of Victorian parents. The thousands of case histories compiled by Kinsey are the direct descendants of Ellis's compassionate and moving biographies of inverts and other deviants. Both men were controversial for making homosexuality and women's sexual pleasure part of the popular discourse about sex. Kinsey's research was crippled by that anti-communist troglodyte Joseph McCarthy (Jesse Helms in a former life) whose slurs and threatened investigations cost Kinsey some major funding.

3 & 4. LEOPOLD VON SACHER-MASOCH and TIM BUCKLEY
   Leopold von Sacher-Masoch, the author of *Venus in Furs,* a classic novel about hapless, submissive Severin's quest for a dominant woman, was shocked and surprised when his name became the root for a new term of algolagniacs. He should be invited to the party anyway and seated — on the floor, of course — next to Tim Buckley, the songwriter and singer whose suicide in the 1970s tragically prevented his recording any more albums like *Greetings from L.A.* "Whip me, beat me, spank me, mama

make it right again," Buckley pleads in one song with tragic force. This work remains *the* rock-and-roll tribute to masochism, dominant black women, cunnilingus, and girls who get off on top.

5. JOSEPHINE BUTLER

Josephine Butler was a middle-class Victorian lady who breached the bounds of good taste to campaign for repeal of the Contagious Diseases Act. The first of these heinous laws was passed in England in 1864. The Acts allowed police to indefinitely detain any woman suspected of being a "common prostitute," subject her to a forced medical exam for venereal disease, and detain her indefinitely if the doctors believed she was infected. At the time, medical science was too backward to accurately diagnose gonorrhea or syphillis — let alone cure them.

Healthy women were often infected by the instruments, which were not washed between examinations. Audiences used to faint when Butler would brandish a speculum and demand that doctors stop raping women with "the steel phallus." She definitely had mistress potential.

6. GAIL PHETERSON

Here is another non-prostitute who nevertheless has devoted her life to campaigning on their behalf. Pheterson is the author of *The Whore Stigma: Female Dishonor and Male Unworthiness* and co-director of the International Committee for Prostitutes Rights in the Netherlands. Her intelligence and zeal should win Pheterson a place in the Sex Radicals' Hall of Fame.

7 & 8. HENRY SPENCER ASHBEE and Mrs. THERESA BERKLEY.

I will seat myself between the good friends Henry Spencer Ashbee and Mrs. Theresa Berkley. Ashbee was a tireless collector of erotica and donated most of his collection to the British Museum upon his death in 1900. Under the pseudonym Pisanus Fraxi, he compiled an exhaustive, wittily annotated index of sexy books, *Notes on Curious and Uncommon Books,* which was published in three volumes from 1877 to 1885. Mrs. Berkley was an infamous Victorian madam who birched some of the most distinguished behinds on the Continent in her lavish establishment at No. 28 Charlotte St., Portland Place. She invented the Berkley Bench, also known as the Berkley Horse, a piece of abusive furniture upon which a male patron could be strapped face down with his genitals dangling through a hole in the bench. He was thus vulnerable to being abused or pleasured at either end. Several pornographic classics are dedicated to or based upon the life of Mrs. Berkley, including the quaintly titled *Venus School-Mistress; or Birchen Sports*, published about 1810.

9 & 10. RICHARD VON KRAFFT-EBING and ROBERT J. STOLLER.

Two of my least favorite people, Richard von Krafft-Ebing, author of *Psychopathia Sexualis* (1882), and Robert J. Stoller, M.D., author of *Perversion: The Erotic Form of Hatred* (1975), will be invited to the dinner party. However, at the door, they will be shackled, gagged, forcibly cross-dressed, anally plugged, catheterized, and forced to wait table. After the dinner party, we'll hook them up to my Relaxacisor and play a little game of truth or dare. I've always wanted to interrogate these supercilious, judgmental, prurient medical experts about the details of their own supposedly perversion-free sex lives.

Leopold and Tim will be jealous, but you can't make an omelet without breaking eggs.

11 PIRATES BELIEVED TO HAVE BEEN HOMOSEXUAL

1. BALDASARRE COSSA (c. 1370–1419)

Before entering the service of the Church and becoming the antipope John XXIII, Cossa was a pirate.

2. BARTHOLOMEW SHARP (fl. 1680)

A sixteen-year-old Spanish boy jumped ship and complained to the Spanish ambassador in London that Sharp had sodomized him.

3 & 4. CHENG I and CHANG PAO (1783–1822)

This pair of Chinese pirates operated in the South China Sea. Cheng I kidnapped Chang Pao, the fifteen-year-old son of a fisherman, and made the youth his lover, then his adopted son. After Cheng's death, Chang Pao took over and proceeded to terrorize all of southeast China, hoping to become emperor. His campaign stalled, however, when his men surrendered, lured by the promise of pardon by the governor of Canton. He eventually became a colonel in the Chinese army.

5. BLACKBEARD (EDWARD TEACH) (d. 1718)

Whenever capturing a ship and its crew, Blackbeard's practice was to save the males and throw the women overboard. Blackbeard married, but his wife's dissatisfaction with him was so well known that a popular song of the day referred to it.

6. LONG BEN (CAPT. JOHN AVERY)

His nickname didn't refer to his height.

7. GEORGE ROUNSIVIL

Although no direct records of Rounsivil's sexual life have survived, his death was revealing. His ship was caught in a storm and broke up on the rocks. Rounsivil escaped in a smaller boat with several other men, but looking back, he saw his companion still aboard the ship. Rounsivil jumped into the water and swam back to the ship in a desperate attempt to rescue his friend, but they both perished.

8. WILLIAM DAMPIER (early 18th century)

In 1690, Dampier purchased a boy named Jeoly, of whom he clearly became very enamored.

9 & 10. ANNE BONNEY (fl. 1718) AND MARY READ (b. 1690)

Though each of these women was married a number of times, they were most likely lovers. They were convicted of piracy in 1720, but managed to escape hanging — Bonney by claiming to be pregnant.

Anne Bonney (left) and Mary Read cut a bloody swath through the Caribbean before they were captured in 1720.

11. GEORGE SHELVOCKE

Shelvocke promoted his cabin boy, Matthew Stuart, to the position of first mate. One disgruntled sailor mused about "what rare qualifications Shelvocke could discover in a fellow, who but a few days before rinsed our glasses and filled us our wine." The crew put up with this, but when Shelvocke drank more than his share of the ship's alcohol supply, a mutiny ensued.

6 NOTEWORTHY SAINTS

1. ST. JOHN THE EVANGELIST (the Apostle) is also known as the Beloved Disciple "whom Jesus loved" and who lay on Jesus' bosom at the Last Supper (John 13:23). Medieval sculptures of John asleep with his head in Christ's lap gave rise to mystical texts in which John is said to have enjoyed the milk of the Lord.

2. ST. SEBASTIAN has been venerated by homosexuals since at least the second half of the nineteenth century, as well as by male artists looking for an excuse to draw a nude male body.

3 & 4. ST. SERGIUS and ST. BACCHUS were said to have been lovers.

5. ST. AELRED OF RIEVAULX, of twelfth-century England, left writings expressing "deep feeling for male spiritual friendship." To control his "carnal impulse," Aelred fasted and took icy baths.

6. ST. MOSES THE HUNGARIAN lived in Russia early in the eleventh century. He was sold as a slave to a Polish noblewoman who developed a yen for him, but he preferred to stay with his fellow Russian prisoners rather than marry her. Angered by his refusal, she finally had Moses whipped and his genitals cut off. He eventually entered a monastery, where he constantly warned the other monks to avoid women and sin. He was canonized by the Russian Orthodox Church.

5 STEPS IN THE GAY APOSTOLIC SUCCESSION

More aptly phrased "the cosmic daisy chain" by writer Martin Greif, this progression has been proudly advertised by its middle link, Gavin Arthur, grandson of President Chester Arthur.

1. WALT WHITMAN slept with

2. EDWARD CARPENTER, who slept with

3. GAVIN ARTHUR, who slept with

4. NEAL CASSADY, who slept with

5. ALLEN GINSBERG

73 HOMOSEXUAL AND BISEXUAL RULERS, AND WHEN THEY RULED

1. King ALEXANDER THE GREAT of Greece, 336–323 B.C.

2. King DEMETRIUS POLIORCETES of Greece, 294–288 B.C.

3. King ANTIOCHUS I of Greece, 280–261 B.C.

4. King ANTIGONUS II GONATAS of Greece, 276–239 B.C.

5. King PTOLEMY IV of Greece, 221–205 B.C.

6. Emperor GAOZU of China, 206–194 B.C.

7. King PTOLEMY VII of Greece, 145–144 B.C.

8. Emperor WU of China, 140–86 B.C.

9. King NICOMEDES IV of Bithynia, early first century B.C.

10. JULIUS CAESAR, consul of Rome, 60–44 B.C.

11. Emperor AUGUSTUS of Rome, 31 B.C. to A.D. 14

12. Emperor AI of China, 6 B.C.–A.D. 1

13. Emperor TIBERIUS of Rome, A.D. 14–37

14. Emperor CALIGULA of Rome, 37–41

15. Emperor CLAUDIUS I of Rome, 41–54

16. Emperor NERO of Rome, 54–68

17. Emperor OTHO of Rome, January–April 69

18. Emperor DOMITIAN of Rome, 81–96

19. Emperor NERVA of Rome, 96–98

20. Emperor TRAJAN of Rome, 98–117

21. Emperor HADRIAN of Rome, 117–138

22. Emperor COMMODUS of Rome, 180–192

23. Emperor HELIOGABALUS of Rome, 218–222

24. Emperor WEI WEN of China, 220–227

25. Emperor JIN DIYI of China, 336–371

26. Emperor VALENTIAN III of Rome, 425–455

27. Emperor LIAN JIANWEN of China, 550–551

28. Emperor CONSTANTINE V of the Byzantine Empire, 741–775

29. Emperor MICHAEL III of the Byzantine Empire, 842–867

30. AL-HAKEM II, ruler of Córdoba (Spain), 961–976

31. HISHAM II, ruler of Córdoba (Spain), 965–1013

32. Emperor BASIL II of the Byzantine Empire, 976–1025

33. SEBÜKTIGIN, founder of the Ghaznavid Empire (Afghanistan), tenth century

34. Emperor MAHMUD of Ghazni (Afghanistan), 997–1030

35. Emperor CONSTANTINE VIII of the Byzantine Empire, 1025–1028

36. Emperor CONSTANTINE IX of the Byzantine Empire, 1042–1055

37. AL-MUTAMID, ruler of Seville (Spain), 1069–1090

38. King WILLIAM II of England, 1087–1100

39. King RICHARD I (THE LION-HEARTED) of England, 1198–1199

40. Holy Roman Emperor FREDERICK II, 1212–1250

41. King EDWARD II of England, 1307–1327

42. ASHIKAGA YOSHIMITSU, shogun of Japan, 1368–1394

43. Sultan BEYAZID I of the Ottoman Empire, 1389–1402

44. King JUAN II of Castile and León (Spain), 1406–1454

45. King ENRIQUE IV of Castile (Spain), 1454–1474

46. Sultan MEHMED (MUHAMMAD) II of the Ottoman Empire, 1451–1481

47. King CHARLES IX of France, 1560–1574

48. ODA NOBUNAGA, military dictator of Japan, 1568–1582

49. King HENRI III of France, 1574–1589

50. Holy Roman Emperor RUDOLF II of Germany, 1576–1612; king of Bohemia (Czechoslavakia), 1575–1611; king of Hungary, 1572–1608

51. King JAMES I of England, 1603–1625; king of Scotland (as James IV), 1567–1625

52. Emperor JAHANGIR of India, 1605–1627

53. King LOUIS XIII of France, 1610–1643

54. TOKUGAWA IEMITSU, shogun of Japan, 1622–1651

55. Queen CHRISTINA of Sweden, 1632–1654

56. TOKUGAWA TSUNAYOSHI, shogun of Japan, 1680–1709

57. King WILLIAM III of England, 1689–1702

58. King CHARLES XII of Sweden, 1697–1718

59. Queen ANNE of England, 1702–1714

60. Empress ANNA IOANNOVNA of Russia, 1730–1740

61. FREDERICK II (THE GREAT) of Prussia, 1740–1786

62. Empress CATHERINE II (THE GREAT) of Russia, 1762–1796

63. CHRISTIAN VII of Denmark, 1766–1808

64. KAMRAN, emir of Afghanistan, early nineteenth century

65. King CHARLES XV of Sweden, 1859–1872

66. King LUDWIG II of Bavaria, 1864–1886

67. King ABD AL-RAHMAN of Afghanistan, 1880–1901

68. King MWANGA of Buganda (Uganda), 1884–1897

69. King GUSTAVUS V of Sweden, 1907–1950

70. King FERDINAND I of Bulgaria, 1908–1918

71. King RAMA VI of Thailand, 1910–1925

72. King AMANULLAH KHAN of Afghanistan, 1919–1929

73. President MANUEL AZAÑA of Spain, 1931–1933, 1936–1939

3 SCANDALS THAT SHOOK GOVERNMENTS

1. THE CLEVELAND STREET SCANDAL

In 1889, police raided a male brothel at 19 Cleveland Street in London's West End. The two owners were arrested, but because of a cover-up instigated by the royal family, the brothel's aristocratic clients went unprosecuted.

Lord Arthur Somerset, a close friend of the Prince of Wales, fled the country and spent the rest of his life in France. Prince Albert Victor, second in line to the throne, intervened to protect Somerset and other noblemen.

Even at the time, the public was aware that something was going on, although details were scarce. The government's leading prosecutor wanted to pursue the case, but was held back by cabinet officials. A newspaper printed court testimony implicating the earl of Euston, and was promptly slapped with a lawsuit. Documents that were kept secret until 1975 reveal that other aristocrats bribed some of the callboys and took them abroad, so that they would be unavailable as witnesses.

2. THE EULENBERG AFFAIR

From late 1906 to 1909, the German press was filled with news of an ongoing scandal that has become known as the Eulenberg affair. It centered around Philipp Prince zu Eulenberg-Hertefeld, a close personal friend and advisor to Kaiser Wilhelm.

In 1906, seeking to break Eulenberg's influence over the kaiser, right-wing editor Maximilian Harden publicly charged

Eulenberg and another high-ranking official with homosexuality — a serious crime under German law. Harden further charged that a French diplomat had infiltrated this homosexual circle, and was gathering confidential information that was of use to France. Criminal trials, libel suits, and countersuits followed, all reported in great detail by the press. Rumors even circulated that the kaiser and Eulenberg had been sexually involved.

When the dust finally cleared, three years later, Eulenberg had been ruined. With his moderating influence gone, advocates of "preventive war" soon dominated the government; World War I and the abdication of the kaiser were direct consequences. Harden, when he realized years later what had come of his revelations, confessed that he regretted ever having made them.

While the story broke, the Eulenberg affair received press coverage as sensational as the Watergate affair. Yet within a decade, German historians had all but forgotten what they found to be a distasteful chapter in their country's history.

For gay people, the scandal had mixed results. It reinforced the association of homosexuality with public disgrace. Yet, like the Oscar Wilde trial a decade earlier and the AIDS epidemic today, it focused attention on a long-ignored subject. Many people recognized their own homosexuality for the first time. The affair even gave them a neutral term for themselves: The word *homosexual,* although coined four decades earlier, came into popular usage only because of the Eulenberg affair.

3. RONALD REAGAN'S OFFICE SEX RING

In 1967, Ronald Reagan was the newly elected governor of California, head of the the GOP's conservative wing, and an aspiring but unannounced contender for the 1968 Republican nomination for president.

A split developed within Reagan's inner circle between advocates of a low-key campaign for the nomination, and those pushing for an all-out drive. Press secretary Lyn Nofziger, the leader of the "hawks," sought a way to purge some of his rivals within the governor's mansion. When he heard rumors that one such rival was homosexual, he seized his opportunity.

For six months or longer, Nofziger and his allies tried to document the existence of a "homosexual ring" involving eight moderate Reagan appointees. They gathered circumstantial evidence about several, including Jack Kemp, but no hard proof. Reagan remained in the dark about this palace intrigue until Nofziger's gang gave him their report in October. Within days, two aides had resigned.

Several national reporters knew about all this, but considered the matter closed. Not so for muckraking columnist Drew Pearson. Pearson, a liberal homophobe, saw a chance to go after two favorite targets. In his column of October 31, 1967, he succinctly reported that "a homosexual ring has been operating in [Reagan's] office." He charged that eight men were involved in the ring, and that Reagan had not dismissed any of them until six months after learning of the situation.

Reagan at first denied everything. After the facts were confirmed by others, the governor explained that he had disguised the truth because "I refuse to participate in trying to destroy human beings with no factual evidence."

Pearson gloated that he had "pretty well knocked Reagan out of the box as a Republican candidate." He died two years later, before having a chance to see that time would prove him wrong.

13 FIRES AND CONFLAGRATIONS

1. SAPPHO'S POETRY

Admirers of Sappho's beautiful love poetry copied it by hand and circulated it for a thousand years, until St. Gregory of Nazianzus ordered it burned in A.D. 380. What little of Sappho's work survived that burning was destroyed in a further burning ordered by church authorities in the eleventh century. Today we can read a small portion of her poems only because of an accidental archeological discovery in 1897.

Emily Dickinson's family
and friends burned many
of her letters to them to
protect her privacy.

2. JEROME DUQUESNOY

Duquesnoy, the official court sculptor in Brussels, was arrested for having sex with two of his young models. Church authorities had him burned at the stake. Many other people suffered the same fate in those days for same-sex behavior; Duquesnoy was simply better known than most.

3. LORD BYRON'S PAPERS

Byron seems to have slept freely with both men and women: History records liaisons with several handsome young Greek men, as well as with his married half-sister. After his death in 1824, the poet's memoirs were considered too scandalous for publication, and were burned.

4. EMILY DICKINSON'S CORRESPONDENCE

Dickinson was guarded about her life, and her family and friends burned much of the correspondence they received from her. Enough information survived in other sources, however, for a biographer to reconstruct two love affairs that Dickinson had with other women, a century after they occurred.

5. Sir RICHARD BURTON'S JOURNALS

Burton established a reputation in many fields: He was the first European to explore many regions of Africa, and the first to translate the explicitly homosexual passages of *The Arabian Nights*. When Burton died in 1890, he was so well known that 100,000 people turned out for his funeral. Burton kept extensive diaries that probably documented an actively bisexual life, but we'll never know for sure. Promptly after his death, his deeply religious wife started a giant bonfire. Into it went every one of his many diaries, as well as a dozen unpublished manuscripts.

6. F. HOLLAND DAY'S PHOTOGRAPHS

In the closing years of the nineteenth century, Day became known for his photography. He generally chose historical subjects. Some of his work, like that of the better-known Wilhelm von Gloeden, featured adolescent youths in settings reminiscent of classical Greece. He raised a ruckus in Boston with his photographs of a staged crucifixion, which featured an undraped Christ. In 1904, a fire destroyed Day's studio, taking with it his equipment and most of his photographs.

7. THE SAGITTA WRITINGS

Under the pseudonym "Sagitta," German anarchist John Henry Mackay wrote several works promoting the cause of man/boy love. The German government declared them immoral in 1909 and ordered them burned. Some copies survived, however, and Mackay furtively re-issued them.

8. *ULYSSES*

When no one else would touch it, Margaret Anderson and her lover Jane Heap published James Joyce's masterpiece, *Ulysses,* in their *Little Review.* The U.S. Post Office burned the four issues in which it appeared.

9. *THE WELL OF LONELINESS*

Hall's 1928 novel about "sexual inversion" was not merely banned in Britain; it was ordered destroyed, and many copies were burned.

10. CHARLOTTE MEW'S POEMS

In 1928, poet Charlotte Mew burned most of her work, then killed herself. Modern scholars believe that she was attempting to destroy all evidence of her lesbianism.

11. THE LIBRARY OF THE INSTITUTE FOR SEXOLOGY

For over three decades, German physician Magnus Hirschfeld argued publicly for gay rights. He founded a museum and library devoted to the objective study of sex. In 1933, Nazi students raided the library, then raided Hirschfeld's apartment. An estimated 12,000 books and 35,000 photographs, including many unpublished and irreplaceable works, were seized. Some went into a gigantic public bonfire on the night of May 10, 1933. Others simply disappeared; historian Jim Steakley, who has researched this period extensively, believes they may still be languishing in a cellar in the Soviet Union or in eastern Germany.

12. THE C.O.C. MEMBERSHIP LIST

In the years before World War II, a vibrant homophile community flourished in Europe. One leading activist was Dr. J.A. Schorer, who began a Dutch group that developed into the C.O.C., the world's largest gay organization. In 1940, as the Nazis began persecuting homosexuals in Holland, a man named Arent van Santhorst memorized the group's entire membership list, which was then burned to prevent it from falling into the hands of Hitler's troops. After the war, the list was reconstructed.

13. WILLA CATHER'S PAPERS

Cather herself burned all copies of her correspondence with Isabelle McClung, the woman who was most likely her lover for fifteen years. After her death in 1947, at her instructions, most of her remaining personal papers were also burned.

24 EXILES AND EMIGRÉS*

1. MARC-ANTOINE MURET (1526–1585)
Muret, a brilliant French philologist and humanist who was once imprisoned for "unnatural vice," fled to Italy to avoid punishment a second time. He was sentenced to death in absentia and burned in effigy.

2 & 3. ELEANOR BUTLER (1739–1829) and SARAH PONSONBY (1755–1831)
Butler and Ponsonby fled Ireland together in 1778. After settling in a cottage near Llangolen, Wales, they became affectionately known as the "Ladies of Llangolen."

4. LORD GEORGE GORDON BYRON (1788–1824)
The English Romantic poet was forced into exile in 1816 after his wife left him and rumors of his homosexuality and of his affair with his half-sister began spreading. After spending several years in Italy, he spent the last few months of his life in Greece, trying to help the Greeks in their struggle for independence from the Turks.

5. COUNT AUGUST VON PLATEN-HALLERMÜND (1796–1835)
A German Romantic poet, Platen became increasingly alienated from his homeland and its literature and spent the last years of his life in Italy.

6. LUIS CERNUDA (1802–1963)
A Spanish poet, Cernuda moved to England, and then to the United States, during his country's civil war. He later settled in Mexico, where he died.

7. EDWARD LEAR (1812–1888)
The English humorist and artist left England in 1837 for Rome,

* This list is derived largely from the *Encyclopedia of Homosexuality*.

where he began a series of close friendships with other artists and visiting aristocrats.

8. KARL HEINRICH ULRICHS (1825–1895)
The German homosexual theorist and activist was exiled twice: once after his homeland of Hanover was annexed by Prussia, known for its harsh anti-homosexual laws, and a second time when, upon the unification of Germany, Prussian law was extended throughout the country. Ulrichs had to leave Munich, where he was then living, and spent his last years in Italy.

9. JOHN ADDINGTON SYMONDS (1840–1893)
Symonds, an English scholar and homosexual theorist, moved to Switzerland for his health and soon discovered that homosexuality need not be a crime.

10. OSCAR WILDE (1856–1900)
After he was released from prison in 1897, Wilde went to France. He died in Paris three years later from an ear infection he contracted in prison.

11. BARON WILHELM VON GLOEDEN (1856–1931)
The German photographer Baron von Gloeden found both the weather and the social climate of Sicily more conducive to his health. There he photographed the male nudes for which he became famous.

12. COUNT JACQUES d'ADELSWÄRD FERSEN (1880–1923)
Arrested at twenty-three for taking photographs of naked schoolboys, Adelswärd Fersen, a French writer and aristocrat, was allowed to go into exile for several years on the island of Capri, where he lived with his boy lover.

13. NATALIE BARNEY (1876–1972)
This American writer from Dayton, Ohio, settled in Paris in 1902, where she became a celebrated poet and patron of the arts. Barney wrote most of her works in classic French.

American expatriate Romaine Brooks, like many of her friends, found early twentieth-century Paris to be a haven for lesbians.

14. ROMAINE BROOKS (1874–1970)

Though an American, Brooks was born in Rome and schooled in Geneva, Paris, and Italy. In 1905, she moved to Paris, where she began a successful career as an artist and eventually met her lifelong love, fellow American expatriate Natalie Barney.

15. GERTRUDE STEIN (1874–1946)

The Paris apartment of this experimental American writer became a gathering place for American and English writers as well as for an international *gallerie* of artists.

16. RADCLYFFE HALL (1880–1943)

After the scandal that followed the publication of *The Well of Loneliness,* Hall and her lover, Una Troubridge, judged it more prudent to live abroad. They left England to reside in Paris.

17. SYLVIA BEACH (1887–1962)

After settling in France during World War I, Beach, an American intellectual, established an English-language bookstore and lending library in Paris. Her store, Shakespeare and Company, became an international gathering place for the avant-garde.

18. LUDWIG WITTGENSTEIN (1889–1951)

An Austrian, Wittgenstein was educated at Cambridge but left England to serve in the Austrian army. In 1929, he returned to Cambridge as a research fellow, becoming a professor of philosophy in 1939.

19. KURT HILLER (1885–1972)

The German writer and political activist who pioneered the concept of homosexuals as a minority group, Hiller was arrested by the Nazis in 1933 and beaten almost to death. He escaped to Czechoslovakia, then to England. After the war Hiller returned to Germany, where he tried unsuccessfully to revive the homophile movement.

20. ERNST KANTOROWICZ (1895–1963)

A German historian and Jewish right-wing paramilitarist, Kantorowicz fled the Nazis, ending up in the United States teaching history at Berkeley and Princeton. Later, despite his risky status as a homosexual immigrant, he was one of the few teachers in California to refuse to sign the anti-Communist loyalty oath.

21. THOMAS MANN (1875–1955)

The bisexual German novelist settled in the Los Angeles area after leaving Germany.

22. KLAUS MANN (1906–1949)

The openly homosexual son of Thomas Mann, this German writer aided the U.S. Army in fighting the Nazis after fleeing the Third Reich for America.

23. ANNA FREUD

A closeted lesbian, Freud moved from Vienna to London with her famous father to avoid the Nazis. After his death and the end of the war, she continued living there and became a psychotherapist.

24. CHRISTOPHER ISHERWOOD (1904–1986)
After living in Berlin from 1930 to 1933, the English novelist moved from country to country trying to stay together with his young German lover. He eventually settled in Southern California, where he met the man who would become his lover for the next thirty-three years, the artist Don Bachardy.

9 MASSIVE ANTI-GAY PURGES

1. FOURTEENTH-CENTURY FRANCE
By the early 1300s, the Knights Templar, a medieval Christian military order founded in 1119, had become Europe's greatest international bankers. Deeply in debt to them and wishing to free himself, Philip IV of France had informers denounce the Templars as heretics, blasphemers, and sodomites. Among other crimes, the Templars were accused of forcing initiates, in secret midnight meetings, to kiss members on the buttocks, anus, stomach, navel, and mouth, and then ordering them to commit sodomy. Despite torture that included roasting the victim's feet until the bones fell from their sockets, only two or three confessed to sodomy, while seventy said they were ordered to but did not; in contrast, 123 confessed to spitting at or on the cross during initiation rites. More than 120 died, many burned at the stake.

2. SPAIN AND PORTUGAL UNDER THE INQUISITION
In the infamous courts of the Spanish Inquisition, as well as the secular courts of the time, sodomites were rigorously and routinely flushed out, arrested, tortured, tried. Punishments ranged from banishment to imprisonment and often execution. In Madrid alone, 100 to 150 sodomites were executed; in Valencia, from 1566 to 1775, 50 to 60 of some 350 cases of "crimes against nature" ended at the stake. In Portugal, 4,419 people were accused of or confessed to sodomy, though fewer than 10 percent were arrested and tried, including a disproportionate number of blacks and mulattos, and "only" 30 were actually burned.

3. SEVENTEENTH-CENTURY MEXICO

From 1656 to 1663, under the Spaniards, inquisitors tried to purge homosexuals from Mexico City. Sodomites were garroted and burned in a special area of the city; strangling them first was considered an act of mercy. According to one report, several hundred people came from the city to watch.

4. EIGHTEENTH-CENTURY NETHERLANDS

Protestant persecutors had their day in 1730 in the Netherlands after an edict mandated that sodomites be publicly executed. In a witch-hunt triggered by the discovery of an alleged national network of sodomites, 250 men and boys were convicted. About 70 were strangled to death; the remainder were banished. The following year, 22 men and boys from one area were put to death on a single day after "confessing." Several others were imprisoned for up to sixteen years without a verdict; the prosecutor was later accused of trying to get rid of his political opponents. Altogether about 600 people were prosecuted for sodomy in the Netherlands during the eighteenth century.

5. TWENTIETH-CENTURY ITALY

Mussolini, who hitherto had not regarded homosexuality as a threat to the "virility of the race," began persecuting homosexuals in 1936, after joining with Hitler in the Rome–Berlin Axis. Considered political offenders as of 1938, homosexuals were rounded up in large numbers; several thousand ended up in prison or in exile on remote islands.

6. TWENTIETH-CENTURY GERMANY

There is no firm consensus about the number of individuals who were exterminated by the Nazis for being homosexual. Common estimates range from 5,000 to 15,000. The number could be higher: Nearly 50,000 men were convicted of homosexuality during the twelve years of Nazi rule. Most ended up in concentration camps where, as the lowest of the scapegoats, few survived.

7. TWENTIETH-CENTURY CUBA

After coming to power in 1959, Castro closed all gay establishments. In the next decade, he sent thousands of gays to work camps to prevent them from "contaminating" Cuba's youth. Even today, parents who have homosexual children are required by law to report their "failure" to officials. And among the 125,000 Cubans who left or were deported in the 1980 boatlift to the United States, 10,000 to 20,000 were gay men and lesbians. Cuba mandates HIV testing for everyone, and confines for life anyone found carrying the HIV virus.

8. TWENTIETH-CENTURY ROMANIA

Under Nicolae Ceausescu, any form of homosexuality was strictly forbidden; even an attempt at sex with someone of the same sex could lead to a five-year prison sentence. So pervasive was the secret police network of informants that many gay people, isolated and unable to trust anyone, committed suicide. Homosexuals who were found out faced torture, including shock therapy and castration, and horrific prison conditions.

9. TWENTIETH-CENTURY IRAN

From 1979 to 1984, after the overthrow of the Shah and under the rule of the Ayatollah Khomeini, homosexuals were executed en masse in town squares in Iran. In May 1990, the chief justice of Iran announced a new crackdown on homosexuality and listed five options for homosexuals: being beheaded with a sword, stoned to death, burned alive, buried alive, or hurled from a great height.

Over the course of his lifelong study of homosexuality, Karl Heinrich Ulrichs, the first openly gay person to speak out for homosexual rights, more than doubled his estimate of the proportion of the population that is gay. Even so, his final estimate was only one-twentieth that of Kinsey's figure of ten percent.

8 ESTIMATES OF THE PERCENTAGE OF THE POPULATION THAT IS GAY*

1. ONE IN FIVE HUNDRED
   Estimated by gay rights pioneer Karl Heinrich Ulrichs in 1863

2. ONE IN TWO HUNDRED
   Ulrichs, at a later date (about 1879)

3. ONE AND A HALF TO TWO PERCENT
   Dr. Magnus Hirschfeld, 1904

4. ONE IN TWENTY-TWO
   Dr. Grabowsky, a German writer quoted by Edward Car-

---

* Most of these estimates referred to the adult male population. Some were ambiguous.

penter in *The Intermediate Sex* (1908). Carpenter concluded that these figures "must be exaggerated."

5. ONE IN FIFTY TO ONE IN FIVE HUNDRED
   Dr. Albert Moll, also quoted by Carpenter.

6. TEN PERCENT
   Alfred Kinsey's 1948 estimate of the number of men who were more or less exclusively homosexual for at least three years of their adult life. The study was based on a non-random, self-selected sample of 5300 white males, who were interviewed in depth. Kinsey felt that men found through a random sampling would not talk freely about their experiences, but critics have argued that his figures may be erroneous because heterosexual and homosexual men are probably not equally likely to step forward for a study. There's no agreement, however, as to which side is most likely to be over-represented. Whatever its merits, Kinsey's 10% figure has become the number quoted most widely.

7. TWO PERCENT
   A 1971 survey of male college students by *Playboy* magazine found that 1% indicated an exclusive preference for the same sex and 1% "mostly" preferred the same sex. *Playboy* stressed that it had gone to great lengths to see that the survey was distributed uniformly around the country, but the actual legwork had been left to the magazine's campus representatives, who were not particularly trained in scientific sampling — nor particularly likely to frequent gay hangouts.

8. THREE AND THREE-TENTHS PERCENT
   A 1989 analysis of a Kinsey Institute study conducted in 1970. The survey, which used a random sample of 1450 men, found that 1.4% of them had homosexual experiences "fairly often" during at least some period of their adult lives, and another 1.9% had such experiences "occasionally." Researchers cautioned that these figures should be taken as a minimum, since some respondents probably did not report their experiences accurately.

25 NOTEWORTHY PRACTICES IN OTHER CULTURES

1. BERDACHE

Berdaches — individuals who identified as the opposite sex — were respected, and sometimes feared, in traditional Native American societies, because they were perceived as manifesting a gift from the spirit world. Berdaches were often considered sacred people, honored as healers and shamans, with special ceremonial roles. Male berdaches often specialized in traditional women's skills — basketry, pottery, weaving, bead- and leather-work. Female berdaches sometimes became recognized as warriors and guides, as among the Kutenai of Montana.

2. UNARMED WARRIOR

Among the Cheyenne tribes, men called *hemaneh* sometimes accompanied war parties unarmed and dressed in their best finery. The *hemaneh* would charge the enemy first, alone, galloping at full speed, protected only by his magic, to surprise and frighten the enemy with his fearlessness and trick them into wasting bullets, leaving them defenseless. Scholars believe the *hemaneh* were probably gay.

3. ROPE BABY

Among the Lakota, *koskalaka* are said to be the daughters of a spirit who unites two women in her power. The *koskalaka* dance together, coiling a rope between them to form a "rope baby" that signifies the potency of their relationship. The *koskalaka* are considered to have the power to manipulate physical and nonphysical reality toward specific ends.

4. *WINKTE*

The male counterpart of the *koskalaka,* the *winkte* has been described as being half-man, half-woman, with a gift of prophecy. The Lakota go to a *winkte* to receive a secret name; such names have great power and are not disclosed to strangers.

5. MAYAN COUPLINGS

Gold figurines of men engaged in anal intercourse were carried as "jewels" in Mayan society, and temple art commonly depicted homosexual behavior. Mayan boys typically followed a pattern of becoming the "boy-wife" to an older teenage male, then graduating to being the "husband" of a younger boy, then finally, in their late twenties, marrying a woman. Bisexuality is still the norm among Mayans of the Yucatan.

6. SELF-PROTECTION TRAINING

Among the Inupiaq Eskimo, men grabbing at the genitals and trying to pull down the pants of fully clothed eight- to twelve-year-old boys are following a tradition meant to teach the boys to protect themselves "quickly and calmly."

7. WEDDING NIGHT IN SPARTA

So institutionalized was pederasty in ancient Sparta that when a man married, the unfortunate bride, having cropped her hair for her wedding night, would traditionally lie face down in the dark wearing boy's clothing.

8. BOY-WORSHIP

Some Sufis practiced a meditation known as *shahid bazi,* contemplating, and sometimes embracing or kissing, the face and form of a beloved beardless boy, considered the purest manifestation of God's beauty on earth. Accompanied by music and dance, this practice could lead to ecstatic experiences. Because *shahid bazi* could also lead to unlawful sex, only masters and advanced mystics who were capable of contemplating the irresistible beauty of boys without being seduced were permitted to practice it.

9. FRIDAY NIGHT WITH THE BOYS

Among the Sudanese Mossi tribe, the most beautiful seven- to fifteen-year-old boys were dressed as women and made pages (and sexual partners) of the chief, who was forbidden sexual intercourse with women on Fridays.

10. ROLE REVERSAL
In a pattern contrary to the usual, among the Nkundo peoples of Africa the younger partner penetrated the older one.

11. WEDDING FEASTS
Among the Thonga of South Africa, wedding feasts were held for *nkhonsthana*, "boy-wives," and their elder brothers received the bride-price. At such feasts, the *nkhonsthana* donned wooden breasts and danced, taking them off only when paid to do so by their "husbands."

12. GOOD LUCK RITUAL
Moroccan men, who regard masturbation with horror and fellatio with disgust, believe that a saintly man can transmit some of his religious "good luck" to other men through anal intercourse.

13. THE HIJRAS
The Hijras, an all-male transvestite religious sect in India, worships the Mother Goddess and seeks to identify with her by becoming as feminine as possible. Its members number between 50,000 and 500,000, many of whom surgically remove their penis. Though they are traditionally entertainers and theoretically celibate, some members function as prostitutes, taking the receptive role in intercourse with other men.

14. MALE MARRIAGE
A form of male marriage developed in China's Fujian province during the Ming dynasty (1368–1644). A younger man moved into the household of an older "adoptive brother," whose parents treated him as a son-in-law. Many such marriages lasted twenty years. When family responsibilities demanded that the marriage end, the older husband paid for a suitable bride for the younger.

15. GOLDEN ORCHID ASSOCIATIONS
In nineteenth-century China, exclusively female "Golden Orchid Associations" were common in the Guangzhou province.

Within these groups, lesbian couples could marry, with one partner designated "husband" and the other, "wife." After exchanging ritual gifts the couple held a wedding feast. Later the married couple could adopt young girls, who often inherited property from the couple's parents.

16. *BISU*

Among the Dayak and the Bugis people of Indonesia, androgynous men, or *bisu,* often became religious leaders with great spiritual power, combining masculine and feminine qualities, wearing a mixture of men's and women's clothing, and having sex with men.

17. *GEMBLAKAN*

On Java, powerful men gained social status by lavishing their wealth on a beautiful boy, usually a teenager, taken as a *gemblakan.* The man paid the parents to let him keep the boy for a year or two, and he presented them gifts. Beloved *gemblakan* might stay with the man into their twenties. Because supporting a *gemblakan* has become so expensive, in villages where this tradition continues several men will combine their resources to share a boy, who stays a few days at a time with each group member.

18. THEATER ROLES

Until 1920, *Namsadang* theatre troupes roamed Korea. Comprising forty to fifty homosexual men, each troupe's members were divided into two groups — *Sutdongmo,* or "butches," and *Yodongmo,* "queens." All newcomers had to start as *Yodongmo.*

19. ADULT ADOPTION

In present-day Japan, homosexuality is considered a problem only when it interferes with heterosexual marriage. A socially accepted alternative to marriage is available through adult adoption, which enables same-sex partners to make a legal commitment to one other. When a popular young actor, Oki Masaya, committed suicide in 1983, it was his weeping adoptive "father" whom Japanese television reporters interviewed.

20. S CLUBS

In nineteenth-century Japan, students at girls' schools and women's universities formed "S" clubs, calling themselves "sisters" (using the English word) and meeting in secret to discuss their lesbian feelings.

21. FAMILY ENTERTAINMENT

In the Philippine city of Bacolod, the queen of the local Christmas pageant is usually a gay male transvestite, and drag fashion shows and beauty pageants — often sponsored by civic clubs such as the Kiwanis or Rotary — are popular family entertainment in all parts of the country.

22. TOMBOYS

Filipino lesbians are known as "tomboys" (the English word) and, like gay men, are socially accepted — they may even flirt with neighborhood girls, for example, sending them love notes and little presents without censure — though they can expect some teasing about their "crush" from the girl's parents and neighbors.

23. SEMEN IMPLANTS

Many of the cultures found in the string of islands that make up Melanesia believe that boys naturally lack semen and must be "planted" with semen to become men. Thus, on New Guinea, Keraki boys are ritually sodomized; Onabasulu boys are smeared with semen from masturbating adults; Sambia boys fellate older bachelors (who stop donating semen after they are married for fear of "polluting" the boys with menstrual blood from their wives).

Among the Marind Anim, each boy is assigned an older male partner from whom he receives semen in intercourse, further engaging in homosexual intercourse with multiple partners on ritual occasions. Etoro boys ingest semen from an adult who has been masturbated to orgasm. Group masturbation beside a stream is a key part of the last stages of initiation for Gahuku-Gama males in New Guinea.

24. RITE OF PASSAGE

In the Solomon Islands, lesbian play during a woman's coming-of-age (menstruation) celebration has been reported.

25. OFFICIAL FELLATOR

Most Tahitian villages have a *mahu* who fellates the young men in the village. Traditionally, each village had only one *mahu* at a time; when he died, another would take his place. Nowadays, in some areas, several *mahu* may live near one another.

MIGHTIER THAN THE SWORD

59 GAY AND LESBIAN AUTHORS WHO HAVE WON MAJOR MAINSTREAM AWARDS

1. EDWARD ALBEE
   Pulitzer Prizes for drama: 1975, for *Seascape;* 1967, for *A Delicate Balance*

2. VICENTE ALEIXANDRE (Spanish poet)
   Nobel Prize for Literature, 1977

3. FREDERICK NEWTON ARVIN
   National Book Award, 1951, for *Herman Melville*
   American Academy and Institute of Arts and Letters Award for Literature, 1951

4. W.H. AUDEN
   National Medal for Literature, 1967
   National Book Award, 1956, for *The Shield of Achilles*
   Bollingen Prize in Poetry, 1954
   Pulitzer Prize for poetry, 1948, for *The Age of Anxiety*

5. JAMES BALDWIN
   American Academy and Institute of Arts and Letters Award for Literature, 1956

6. JACINTO BENAVENTE (Spanish dramatist)
   Nobel Prize for Literature, 1922

7. MICHAEL BENNETT, with JAMES KIRKWOOD and NICHOLAS DANTE (plus Marvin Hamlisch, music; and Edward Kleban, lyrics), Pulitzer Prize for drama, 1976, for *A Chorus Line*

8. ELIZABETH BISHOP
   Neustadt International Prize for Literature, 1976
   National Book Critics Circle Award, 1976, for *Geography III*

National Book Award, 1970, for *The Complete Poems*
Fellowship of the Academy of American Poets, 1964
Pulitzer Prize for poetry, 1956, for *Poems— North and South*
American Academy and Institute of Arts and Letters Award for
Literature, 1951

9. MARIE-CLAIRE BLAIS (Canadian)
Prix Médicis, 1966, for *Une Saison dans la vie d'Emmanuel*

10. JOHN BOSWELL
National Book Award, 1981, for *Christianity, Social Tolerance
and Homosexuality*

11. PAUL BOWLES
American Academy and Institute of Arts and Letters Award for
Literature, 1950

12. OLGA BROUMAS
Yale Series of Younger Poets, 1976, for *Beginning with O*

13. JOHN BRUNNER
Hugo Award, 1969, for *Stand on Zanzibar*

14. WILLIAM S. BURROUGHS
American Academy and Institute of Arts and Letters Award for
Literature, 1975

15. TRUMAN CAPOTE
American Academy and Institute of Arts and Letters Award for
Literature, 1959

16. WILLA CATHER
Pulitzer Prize for fiction, 1923, for *One of Ours*

17. ALFRED CORN
Fellowship of the Academy of American Poets, 1987
American Academy and Institute of Arts and Letters Award for
Literature, 1983

18. SAMUEL R. DELANY

  Nebula Awards: 1970, for "Time Considered as a Helix of Semiprecious Stones"; 1968, for *The Einstein Connection;* 1968, for "Aye, and Gomorrah"; 1967, for *Babel-17*

  Hugo Award, 1970, for "Time Considered as a Helix of Semiprecious Stones"

19. ROBERT DUNCAN

  American Book Award, 1985, for *Ground Work: Before the War*

20. ANDRÉ GIDE (French novelist)

  Nobel Prize for Literature, 1947

21. ALLEN GINSBERG

  National Book Award, 1974, for *The Fall of America: Poems of These States, 1965–1971*

  American Academy and Institute of Arts and Letters Award for Literature, 1969

22. PAUL GOODMAN

  American Academy and Institute of Arts and Letters Award for Literature, 1953

23. JUDY GRAHN

  American Book Award, 1983, for *Queen of Wands*

24. SUSAN GRIFFIN

  Emmy Award, 1975, for *Voices*

25. THOM GUNN

  American Academy and Institute of Arts and Letters Award for Literature, 1964

26. MARILYN HACKER

  National Book Award, 1975, for *Presentation Piece*

  Lamont Poetry Selection, 1973, for *Presentation Piece*

27. RICHARD HOWARD
    National Book Award, 1983, for translating *Les Fleurs du Mal,*
    by Baudelaire
    Pulitzer Prize for poetry, 1970, for *Untitled Subjects*
    American Academy and Institute of Arts and Letters Award for
    Literature, 1970

28. LANGSTON HUGHES
    American Academy and Institute of Arts and Letters Award for
    Literature, 1946

29. WILLIAM INGE
    Pulitzer Prize for drama, 1953, for *Picnic*

30. HANS HENNY JAHNN (German dramatist and novelist)
    Kleist Prize, 1919, for *Pastor Ephraim Magnus*

31. MAURICE KENNY
    American Book Award, 1984, for *The Mama Poems*

32. PETER KLAPPERT
    Yale Series of Younger Poets, 1970, for *Lugging Vegetables to
    Nantucket*

33. SELMA LAGERLÖF (Swedish novelist)
    Nobel Prize for Literature, 1909

34. URSULA K. LeGUIN
    National Book Award, 1973, for *The Farthest Shore*
    Nebula Awards: 1975, for *The Dispossessed;* 1975, for "The
    Day before the Revolution"; 1970, for *The Left Hand of
    Darkness*
    Hugo Awards: 1974, for "The Ones Who Walk Away From
    Omelas"; 1973, for *The Word for World Is Forest;* and 1970,
    for *The Left Hand of Darkness*

35. AMY LOWELL
    Pulitzer Prize for poetry, 1926, for *What's O'Clock*

36. THOMAS MANN (German novelist)
    Nobel Prize for Literature, 1929

37. CARSON McCULLERS
    American Academy and Institute of Arts and Letters Award for
    Literature, 1943

38. EDNA ST. VINCENT MILLAY
    Pulitzer Prize for poetry, 1923, for *The Ballad of the Harp-
    Weaver and Other Poems*

39. WILLIAM MEREDITH
    Academy of American Poets Fellowship, 1990
    Pulitzer Prize for poetry, 1988, for *Partial Accounts: New and
    Selected Poems*
    American Academy and Institute of Arts and Letters Award for
    Literature, 1958
    Yale Series of Younger Poets, 1943, for *Love Letter from an
    Impossible Land*

40. JAMES MERRILL
    National Book Critics Circle Award, 1983, for *The Changing
    Light at Sandover*
    National Book Awards: 1979, for *Mirabell: Books of Number;*
    1967, for *Nights and Days*
    Bollingen Prize in Poetry, 1971–1972
    Pulitzer Prize for poetry, 1977, for *Divine Comedies*

41. MICHAEL MOORCOCK
    Nebula Award, 1968, for "Behold the Man"

42. MARIANNE MOORE
    National Medal for Literature, 1968
    Fellowship of the Academy of American Poets, 1965
    Pulitzer Prize for poetry, 1952, for *Collected Poems*
    National Book Award, 1952, for *Collected Poems*
    Bollingen Prize in Poetry, 1951

American Academy and Institute of Arts and Letters Award for Literature, 1946

43. CHERRIE MORAGA and GLORIA ANZALDUA
    American Book Award, 1986, for editing *This Bridge Called My Back: Writings by Radical Women of Color*

44. FRANK O'HARA
    National Book Award, 1972, for *The Collected Poems*

45. MINNIE BRUCE PRATT
    Lamont Poetry Selection, 1989, for *Crime against Nature*

46. REYNOLDS PRICE
    National Book Critics Circle Award, 1986, for *Kate Vaiden*
    American Academy and Institute of Arts and Letters Award for Literature, 1971

47. ADRIENNE RICH
    Ruth Lilly Poetry Prize, 1986
    National Book Award, 1974, for *Diving into the Wreck: Poems, 1971–1972*
    American Academy and Institute of Arts and Letters Award for Literature, 1960
    Yale Series of Younger Poets, 1951, for *A Change of World*

48. MURIEL RUKEYSER
    American Academy and Institute of Arts and Letters Award for Literature, 1942
    Yale Series of Younger Poets, 1935, for *Theory of Flight*

49. JOANNA RUSS
    Nebula Award, 1973, for "When It Changed"

50. MAY SARTON
    American Book Award, 1985, for *At Seventy: A Journal*

51. JAMES SCHUYLER
    Fellowship of the Academy of American Poets, 1983
    Pulitzer Prize for poetry, 1981, for *The Morning of the Poem*
    American Academy and Institute of Arts and Letters Award for
    Literature, 1977

52. MAY SWENSON
    Bollingen Prize in Poetry, 1979–1980
    Fellowship of the Academy of American Poets, 1979
    American Academy and Institute of Arts and Letters Award for
    Literature, 1960

53. SARA TEASDALE
    Pulitzer Prize for poetry, 1918, for *Love Songs*

54. JAMES TIPTREE, JR. (ALICE SHELDON)
    Nebula Awards: 1978, for "The Screwfly Solution" (under the
    pseudonym Raccoona Sheldon); 1977, for *Houston, Houston, Do You Read?*; 1974, for "Love is the Plan, the Plan is
    Death"
    Hugo Awards: 1977, for *Houston, Houston, Do You Read?*;
    1974, for *The Girl Who Was Plugged In*

55. EDMUND WHITE
    American Academy and Institute of Arts and Letters Award for
    Literature, 1983

56. PATRICK WHITE (Australian novelist)
    Nobel Prize for Literature, 1973

57. KATE WILHELM
    Nebula Awards: 1988, for "Forever Yours"; 1987, for "The Girl
    Who Fell into the Sky"; 1969, for "The Planners"
    Hugo Award, 1977, for *Where Late the Sweet Birds Sang*

58. TENNESSEE WILLIAMS
    Pulitzer Prizes for drama: 1955, for *Cat on a Hot Tin Roof*;
    1948, for *A Streetcar Named Desire*

American Academy and Institute of Arts and Letters Award for Literature, 1944

59. LANFORD WILSON
Pulitzer Prize for drama, 1980, for *Talley's Folly*
American Academy and Institute of Arts and Letters Award for Literature, 1973

22 EARLY AND LESSER-KNOWN WORKS OF LITERATURE

1. *THE EPIC OF GILGAMESH,* Mesopotamian.
Several thousand years ago, this epic poem told the story of Gilgamesh, king of the Uruks, who was transformed through love for his comrade, Enkidu, into a virtuous ruler.

2. UNTITLED STORY, c. 2300 B.C., Egyptian.
In an ancient short story, King Pepy II Neferkare (2355–2261 B.C.) visits his general Sisinne at night to have sex.

3. *SATYRICON,* by Petronius Arbiter, first century A.D., Greek.
This picaresque work describes the adventures of the narrator and his boyfriend in southern Italy.

4. *LEUCIPPE AND CLITOPHON,* by Achilles Tatius, second century A.D., Greek.
A novel debating the relative merits of boys and women as love objects, interspersed with both heterosexual and homosexual episodes.

5. *MUSA PAIDIKE,* Book XII of the *GREEK ANTHOLOGY* (also known as the Palatine Anthology), compiled by a Byzantine scholar, Constantine Cephalas, in the tenth century, and based on three earlier anthologies.
The poems in Book XII, the core of which were collected in 80

B.C. and which date through the second century, celebrate and detail the Greek practice of pederasty. Because of their explicitness, the complete book of poems was not published until 1764.

6. "GANYMEDE AND HELEN," anonymous, twelfth century, Latin.

In this long poem, Ganymede rebuffs Helen, who has offered herself to him. An argument ensues, mediated by Nature and Reason, over pederasty versus heterosexuality. Heterosexuality wins.

7. Sequel to *HUON OF BORDEAUX,* anonymous, 1220, French.

Ide, the granddaughter of Huon, dresses as a knight so that she can do battle on the side of the Holy Roman Emperor's forces. The emperor rewards Ide's prowess by giving her his daughter, Olive, to marry. Ide cannot refuse, so she pleads illness on their wedding night, and tries to satisfy her new bride by "clyppynge and kyssynge" throughout the eight-day wedding feast. It's not enough. Ide finally confesses to her unhappy bride, and the emperor decrees that she shall be burned. Ide is miraculously saved at the last minute when she is transformed into a man.

8. *RECORDS OF THE CUT SLEEVE,* anonymous, fifteenth century, Chinese.

This anonymous collection of homosexual vignettes was collected during the Ming dynasty (1368–1644) from sources spanning almost two millenia. It was the first history of Chinese homosexuality and perhaps the first comprehensive history of homosexuality in any culture.

9. *ESSAYS IN IDLENESS,* by Yoshida Kenko, fourteenth-century, Japanese.

A courtier-monk describes his sexual attraction to boys.

10. *CANTICI DI FIDENZIO,* by Camillo Scroffa, 1562, Italian.

A collection of satirical love poetry supposedly written by an "amorous pedant" who is haplessly in love with a handsome pupil; tender and candid despite its satire. Initiated a minor genre of poetry in Italy.

11. *L' ALCIBIADE FANCIULLO A SCOLA [Alcibiades the School-boy]*, by Antonio Rocco, 1652, Italian.

In this story, a sexually explicit defense of pederasty set in ancient Athens, a lustful teacher argues socratically to overcome a reluctant pupil's objections to consummation of their relationship. Though it was published anonymously, the work is attributed to Antonio Rocco, a libertine priest and Aristotelian philosopher.

12. *THE GREAT MIRROR OF MALE LOVE,* by Ihara Saikaku, 1687, Japanese.

A collection of short stories about love between samurai and their pages and between kabuki actor–prostitutes and their patrons.

13. *MARY, A FICTION,* by Mary Wollstonecraft, 1788.

Wollstonecraft, an early feminist, based this novel on her real-life "consuming attachment" to Fanny Blood.

14. *EROS: Die Männerliebe der Griechen,* compiled by Heinrich Hoessli, 1836–1838, German.

An anthology that includes many homosexual selections from ancient and Islamic verse.

15. *PINHUA BAOJIAN [A Mirror Ranking Precious Flowers]*, mid-nineteenth century, Chinese.

A literary masterpiece that details the romances of male actors and their patrons.

16. *NOODLOT,* by Louis Couperus, 1891, Dutch.

In this novel, Bertie, who loves Frank, sabotages Frank's marriage to a woman. When Bertie confesses, years later, Frank kills him. After his release from prison, Frank and his fiancée wed, but the marriage is never a happy one. *Noodlot* was one of several novels by Couperus with homoerotic undertones.

17. *O BOM CRIOULO,* by Adolfo Caminha, 1895, Brazilian.
This novel about a love affair between a cabin boy and his black protector has recently been been translated into English.

18. *AT SAINT JUDAS'S,* by Henry Blake Fuller, ca. 1896, American.
This short play about a homosexual who kills himself at the wedding of his former lover, though poorly written, was the first American play to deal explicitly with homosexuality.

19. *WHITE STAINS,* by Aleister Crowley, 1898, British.
A collection of verse in which the eccentric Crowley extols the joys of pederasty.

20. *LIEBLINGMINNE UND FREUNDESLIEBE IN DER WELT-LITERATUR [The Love of Comrades and Friends in World Literature],* compiled by Elisàr von Kupffer, 1900, German.
The first true anthology of male homosexuality.

21. *WINGS,* by Mikhail Alekseevich Kuzmin, 1906, Russian.
Kuzmin's portrait of a young homosexual caused a great scandal in its day.

22. *O 3° SEXO,* by Odilon Azevedo, 1930, Brazilian.
Brazil's first and most outspoken lesbian (and radical feminist) novel, in which lesbian workers organize to oust men from power.

18 GAY AND LESBIAN PERIODICALS PUBLISHED BEFORE 1960

1. *URANUS*
Karl Heinrich Ulrichs began this periodical for "Urnings" in 1870, after four years of planning. It died after a single issue for lack of support.

2. *DER EIGENE: Ein Batt für mannliche Kultur [The Exceptional: A Magazine for Male Culture]*
   The world's first successful homosexual periodical. When begun in 1896 its subtitle was "Monthly for Art and Life," but in 1899, after the Scientific-Humanitarian Committee was founded, the subtitle was changed to openly declare the magazine's focus. Adolf Brand edited it from its beginning to its end, in 1931, and the homoerotic literature and art that filled its pages reflected his own idealization of the pederastic tradition.

3. *JAHRBUCH FÜR SEXUELLE ZWISCHENSTUFEN MIT BE-SONDERER BERÜCKSICHTIGUNG DER HOMOSEXUALITÄT [Yearbook for Sexual Intermediates with Special Reference to Homosexuality]*
   This was the world's first journal of scholarship on homosexuality. It was published annually from 1899 to 1923 by the Scientific-Humanitarian Committee, and edited by Magnus Hirschfeld, the founder of the committee and the leader of the homosexual rights movement in Germany. Encompassing scholarly articles, reviews of the literature then available about homosexuality, and commentary on current events, its twenty-three volumes are today still of unique value to serious students of homosexuality.

4. *DIE FREUNDSCHAFT [Friendship]*
   The German Friendship Association began publishing this as a weekly in 1920; in 1923 they made it a monthly, with a focus on literature and culture.

5. *DIE FREUNDIN [The Girlfriend]*
   This German magazine, published in the late 1920s and early 1930, openly discussed lesbian issues.

6. *URANOS*
   This was another German literary and cultural journal being published in the 1920s.

7. *FRIENDSHIP AND FREEDOM*

The Chicago Society for Human Rights published only two issues of this newspaper before dissolving in 1925.

8. *INVERSIONS*

Publication of this French journal was halted in 1925 after only a few issues when the publisher was prosecuted and convicted.

9. *DER KREIS/LE CERCLE*

A lesbian known as Mammina began this monthly journal (and its sponsoring club) in 1933 under the name *Schweizerisches Freundschaftsblatt [Swiss Friendship Bulletin]*. In 1943, after Mammina turned the reins over to a gay man, the club became all-male and the magazine's name was changed to *Der Kreis*. Karl Meier (aka "Ralf") edited it, publishing articles, short stories, and photographs aimed at the general gay reader. After French and English sections were added, in 1943 and 1952 respectively, it became very much an international journal. Among those whose work appeared in its pages were the photographer George Platt Lynes, the artist Paul Cadmus, and the writers James Barr and Samuel M. Steward (under various pseudonyms). The magazine and the club folded in 1967.

10. *LEVENSRECHT [Right to Live]*

This Dutch magazine was founded in 1940 and folded the same year, at the outbreak of war with Germany. Though its editors tried to revive it in 1946, the police succeeded in stopping its publication.

11. *VRIENDSCHAP [Friendship]*

The newly formed Shakespeare Club, founded by the editors of Levensrecht, began this magazine in 1946, and for some reason the Dutch authorities, which had just shut down *Levensrecht,* left *Vriendschap* alone. It was still publishing over four decades later, as a monthly lesbian magazine under the name *Lesbisch-en Homoblad.*

12. *PAN-BLADET*
Founded in the late 1940s or early 1950s, this Danish newspaper is still publishing, with a circulation of 10,000.

13. *VICE VERSA*
In 1947, a woman calling herself Lisa Ben (an anagram of *lesbian*) began the first American publication by and for lesbians. She published a total of nine issues, which included poetry; short stories; editorials; reviews of plays, books, and films; and an annotated bibliography of novels of interest to lesbians.

14. *VENNEN [Friends]*
The Danish Forbundet af 1948 founded this periodical in 1949.

15. *ONE MAGAZINE: The Homosexual Viewpoint*
ONE was founded in 1952 by members of the Mattachine Society but published independently of the Society. A monthly, it was the first gay magazine in the U.S. to reach a wide audience — 5,000 readers at its peak — though the publishers had to go to the Supreme Court to get the local postmaster to let them distribute through the U.S. mails. *ONE* reported on entrapment and harassment cases, as well as printing intellectual and cultural articles. Many of its writers published under pseudonyms — both to protect their identities and to make the staff look larger than it was. It stopped regular publication in 1969.

16. *ARCADIE*
Founded in 1953 by André Baudry, who also served as its editor, this French monthly began as an offshoot of *Der Kreis*. For many years it was the most intellectual of the periodicals promoting gay rights, and it was noted for the high quality of its scholarly articles.

17. *MATTACHINE REVIEW*
More restrained in its advocacy of gay activism than *ONE* and somewhat more scholarly, the *Mattachine Review* was begun in January 1955 after a reorganization of the Mattachine Society. As

the organ of the society, it lost its support when the society dissolved, and ceased publishing in 1964.

18. *THE LADDER*
   The newly formed Daughters of Bilitis founded this monthly publication in 1956. Consciously kept nonpolitical, it was aimed at the individual lesbian, especially "the lonely isolated lesbians away from the big cities." Contents included poetry, fiction, history, biography, and articles addressing such matters as raising children in a lesbian household or coping with heterosexual marriage. At the end of 1962, Barbara Gittings took over the editorship and the magazine became more outspokenly political. Feminism became a dividing issue in 1968 when Barbara Grier became editor and Rita Laporte became president of DOB, and in 1970 Grier and Laporte split off from DOB and began publishing *The Ladder* independently. When financial difficulties forced an end to its publication in 1972, it was the oldest continuously published gay periodical in the U.S.

22 PENNAMES AND PSEUDONYMS — AND WHO THEY REALLY WERE

1. PHIL ANDROS: Samuel M. Steward

2. BRYHER: Annie Winifred Ellerman

3. DONALD WEBSTER CORY: Edward Sagarin

4. GENE DAMON: Barbara Grier

5. HADRIAN: Fitzroy Davis

6. NIAL KENT: William Leroy Thomas

7. BILL LAMBERT: Dorr Legg

8. RICHARD MEEKER: Forman Brown

9. XAVIER MAYNE: Edward I. Stevenson

Writer Samuel Steward, aka Phil Andros, took his pseudonym from the Greek words for "love" and "man."

10. ISABEL MILLER: Alma Routsong

11. CLAIRE MORGAN: Patricia Highsmith

12. NUMA NUMANTIUS: Karl Heinrich Ulrichs

13. DR. RAMIEN: Magnus Hirschfeld

14. MARY RENAULT: Mary Challans

15. A.N. ROQUELAIRE: Anne Rice

16. STEN RUSSELL: Stella Rush

17. SAGITTA: John Henry Mackay

18. SAKI: Hector Hugh Munro

19. SANDY SAUNDERS: Helen Sandoz

20. JAMES TIPTREE, Jr.: Alice Sheldon

21. TRYPHÉ: Natalie Barney

22. D.B. VEST: Gerald Heard

22 NOTEWORTHY WORKS ABOUT AIDS

1. *ONE*, by Jeffrey Hagedorn, 1983. This one-man, one-act play premiered in Chicago in August 1983 with Carl Forsberg in the single role. It was the first play about AIDS.

2. *AS IS*, by William Hoffman, 1985. Hoffman's groundbreaking play received strong praise from most critics.

3. *HOT LIVING*, edited by John Preston, 1985. The first book of erotic safer-sex stories.

4. *THE NORMAL HEART*, Larry Kramer, 1985. Kramer's play about a gay journalist crusading for a response to the AIDS crisis was staged in L.A. with Richard Dreyfuss in the lead.

5. *THE SCREAMING ROOM*, by Barbara Peabody, 1986. A mother's powerful memoir.

6. *GOOD-BYE, I LOVE YOU*, by Carol Lynn Pearson, 1986. A wife's memoir.

7. *TWEEDS*, by Clayton R. Graham, 1987. A "serio-comic" novel.

8. *NIGHT KITES*, by M.E. Kerr. Excellent young-adult fiction.

9. *A QUIET END*, by Robin Swados, 1988. This play premiered in St. Louis.

10. *THE DARKER PROOF*, by Adams Mars-Jones and Edmund White, 1988. Short stories.

11. *VALLEY OF THE SHADOW*, by Christopher Davis, 1988. An eloquent novel, written as a memoir.

12. *AT RISK*, by Alice Hoffman, 1988. Hoffman's novel received wide mainstream attention, but was criticized by many activists for trying to hop on the bandwagon while missing the real issues.

13. *SECOND SON*, by Robert Ferro, 1988. Well-written fiction by a gay writer who died of AIDS soon afterward.

14. *GROUND ZERO,* by Andrew Holleran, 1988. Essays by the author of *Dancer from the Dance.*

15. *BORROWED TIME: An Aids Memoir,* by Paul Monette, 1988. The author's moving, prize-winning portrayal of his life with Paul Horowitz, who died in 1986.

16. *LOVE ALONE: Eighteen Elegies For Rog,* by Paul Monette, 1988. Eloquent poetry that complements *Borrowed Time.*

17. *MORTAL EMBRACE: Living with AIDS,* by Emmanuel Dreuilhe, 1988. Memoirs of a French PWA.

18. *MORE THAN NAMES,* by David Lemos, 1988. A play based on the Names Project AIDS Memorial Quilt.

19. *STRIP AIDS U.S.A.,* edited by Trina Robbins, Bill Sienkiewicz, and Robert Triptow, 1988. Cartoons about AIDS.

20. *THE IRREVERSIBLE DECLINE OF EDDIE SOCKET,* by John Weir, 1989. A black comedy novel about AIDS.

21. *POETS FOR LIFE,* by Michael Klein, 1989. Seventy-six poets address AIDS in this powerful and varied anthology.

22. *AFTERLIFE,* by Paul Monette, 1990. A novel about "AIDS widowers," by the author of *Borrowed Time.*

7 REASONS AUTHORS HAVE GIVEN TO ALYSON PUBLICATIONS FOR NOT DEALING WITH AIDS OR SAFER SEX IN THEIR NOVELS, AND THE YEARS WE HEARD THEM

1. "What's AIDS?" (1983)

2. "It's set in the future, in 1990, when there's a vaccine." (1984)

3. "It's set in Europe, where AIDS isn't much of a problem." (1985)

4. "It's set in the recent past, before AIDS was known." (1984, 1985, 1986, 1987, 1988, 1989, 1990)

5. "All the main characters have been tested and they're all HIV-negative." (1986)

6. "It would mess up the pacing." (1986)

7. "It's set in the future, in the year 2000, when there's a vaccine." (1988)

31 FICTIONAL DETECTIVES*

1. CAROL ASHTON
   This lesbian police detective, attractive and successful, lives in Sydney, Australia. In Claire McNab's *Lessons in Murder* (1988), Ashton investigates the murder of a schoolteacher and falls in love with her prime suspect. *Fatal Reunion* and *Death Down Under* followed.

2. HELEN BLACK
   Black, a private investigator, is introduced in Pat Welch's *Murder by the Book,* which the author promises is only the first in a series.

3. DAVE BRANDSTETTER
   The grandfather of gay detectives, Brandstetter is actually a Los Angeles insurance agent created by Joseph Hanson and currently appearing in nearly a dozen novels, and several short stories. He is not a gay militant, but lives openly with male lovers, including a black television reporter named Cecil Harris. The

---

* Thanks to Eric Garber for supplying most of this list.

Brandstetter series includes *Fadeout, The Man Everybody Was Afraid Of,* and *Nightwork.*

4. GEOFFRY CHADWICK

This gay, middle-aged, Montreal lawyer is featured in two Edward Phillips's novels: *Sunday's Child* (1981) and *Buried on Sunday* (1988).

5. KATE DELAFIELD

This premiere lesbian detective, working with the L.A.P.D. Homicide Department, is the creation of a premiere lesbian writer, Katherine V. Forrest. Delafield appears in several mystery novels and stories, including *Amateur City*, which introduced the character in 1984; *Murder at the Nightwood Bar,* which is currently optioned to become a major film; and *The Beverly Malibu,* which won a Lammy award as best lesbian mystery.

6. NICK DUFFY

Nick Duffy is a bisexual British investigator. He appears in four Dan Kavanagh novels, starting with *Duffy* (1980).

7. KATERINA GUERRERA

In M.F. Beal's *Angel Dance* (1977), this Chicana lesbian-feminist detective uncovers CIA espionage and corruption while protecting the beautiful feminist author Angel Stone.

8. SOPHIE HOROWITZ

Sophie Horowitz is a lesbian reporter for Manhattan's *Feminist News* when she investigates a missing radical feminist in Sarah Schulman's *The Sophie Horowitz Story* (1984).

9. HELEN KEREMOS

This Canadian lesbian detective is first introduced in Eve Zaremba's *A Reason to Kill* (1978).

10. JAKE LIEBERMAN

Jake Lieberman is a gay detective in Stephen Lewis's *Cowboy Blues* (1985).

11. CHESTER LONG

Carleton Carpenter's 1973 mystery *Only Her Hairdresser Knew* introduces Chester Long, owner of Chet's Hair Stylists in Greenwich Village. It's only one of several novels in which Long makes an appearance.

12. PHAROAH LOVE

Pharoah Love is an amoral cop, a sixties-style swinger, black, and homosexual. He appears in four novels by George Baxt, *A Queer Kind of Death* (1966), *Swing Low, Sweet Harriet* (1967), *Topsy and Evil* (1968), and *The Tallulah Bankhead Murders* (1987), though he's pivotal to only the first two.

13. CORD McGREEVY

When the police find the case too kinky to investigate, this Manhattan schoolteacher takes it upon himself to discover the killer of his former lover in Richard Hall's *The Butterscotch Prince* (1975).

14. MADISON McGUIRE

McGuire, a former intelligence officer, plays detective in Amanda Kyle Williams's *Club Twelve,* and will reappear in future mysteries.

15. STONER McTAVISH

McTavish is the co-owner of a Boston travel agency. A open lesbian, McTavish is single and lives with her palm-reading Aunt Hermione. She first appears in Sarah Dreher's *Stoner McTavish* (1985).

16. CASS MILAM

Amateur detectives come from all walks of life. Cass Milam is a landscape architect, who attacks her first mystery in Antoinette Azolakov's *Cass and the Stone Butch.*

17. FRANCIS MORLEY

What does an effeminate former chorus boy do when he inherits a detective agency? If he's Francis Morley, he hires a butch ex-Marine named Tiger as an assistant, then launches a murder investigation that sends him to gay bars and steamy bathhouses. Morley's sole appearance is in *The Gay Detective* (1961) by Lou Rand.

18. PAM NILSEN

This radical lesbian-feminist works in a Seattle printing collective. She takes on her first case in Barbara Wilson's popular novel, *Murder in the Collective* (1984).

19. LAMAAR RANSOM

Lamaar Ransom is a hard-boiled, wise-cracking, Los Angeles private investigator. She is also a glamorous lesbian with a beautiful Chicana girlfriend and a flamboyant gay black secretary named "Lavender." In David Galloway's *Lamaar Ransom, Private Eye* (1979), Ransom investigates the disappearance of actress Yvette La-Flamme, and discovers treachery, blackmail, and murder.

20. CAITLIN REECE

Caitlin Reece is an experienced Canadian lesbian detective who first appears in Lauren Wright Douglas's *The Always Anonymous Beast* (1987).

21. HENRY RIOS

Rios is a gay Latino lawyer whose legal background helps his sleuthing in Michael Nava's *Little Death* (1986). He reappears in *Goldenboy* (1988), which won the author two Lammy awards, and *Howtown*.

22. TOM RIPLEY

An amoral American living in Europe, Ripley gets involved in a variety of ruthless and usually illegal schemes. He was introduced in a series of Patricia Highsmith's novels beginning with *The Talented Mr. Ripley* in 1957. Though happily married, Ripley is shown to have bisexual capacities, particularly in the 1980 *The Boy Who Followed Ripley*. Other series titles include *Ripley Under Ground* and *Ripley's Game*.

23. MATT SINCLAIR

Matt Sinclair is a bitchy New Orleans antique dealer, occasional lawyer, and reluctant detective. Openly gay, though not a gay activist, Sinclair lives with a much younger lover, Robin. He gets involved in a series of grisly murders in Tony Fennelly's *The Glory Hole Murders* (1985) and *The Closet Hanging* (1987).

24. SUE SLATE

Popular lesbian columnist Lee Lynch introduces this new detective in the Naiad Press book *Sue Slate, Private Eye*.

25. GERTRUDE STEIN and ALICE B. TOKLAS

In real life, Gertrude Stein was a renowned American expatriate, writer, and art patron in the early decades of the century. She and her companion, Alice B. Toklas, become amateur sleuths in Steven Abbott's unclassifiable *Rhino Ritz: An American Mystery* (1979) and again in Samuel M. Steward's *Murder is Murder is Murder* (1985) and *The Caravaggio Shawl* (1989).

26. DON STRACHEY

Albany's only openly gay detective is Don Strachey, who's also a gay activist. He is happily involved with a lover, Timmy, and appears in three Richard Stevenson novels, the first of which is *Death Trick*.

27. DAN VALENTINE

Dan Valentine is a bartender at Bonaparte's, a Boston gay men's bar. Along with his straight woman friend, Clarisse Lovelace, Valentine turns sleuth to investigate a series of crimes, first in Nathan Aldyne's *Vermillion* (1980), followed by *Cobalt, Slate,* and *Canary*.

28. EMMA VICTOR

This lesbian working on the Women's Hotline in Boston gets drawn into a murder in Mary Wing's *She Came Too Late* (1987). She reappears in *She Came in a Flash*.

29. ROSIE VINCENTE

Vincente, a Berkeley-based lesbian carpenter and amateur sleuth, is the partner of Jake Samson, ostensibly the lead character in several Shelley Singer mysteries, including *Samson's Deal*, *Full House*, *Spit in the Ocean*, and *Free Draw*.

30. LYLA WADE

Vicki McConnell has so far written three Lyla Wade mysteries; the first is *Mrs. Porter's Letter*.

31. VIRGINIA WOOLF

Virginia Woolf was a noted British author and member of the Bloomsbury Group. In Ellen Hawkes and Peter Manso's *The Shadow of the Moth* (1983), Woolf investigates a young woman's suicide, gets drawn into a dangerous web of espionage, and finds herself attracted to a female reporter.

MICHAEL DENNENY'S
10 FAVORITE GAY AND LESBIAN BOOKS*

1. *ANOTHER MOTHER TONGUE: Gay Words, Gay Worlds*, by Judy Grahn

An astonishing synthesis that will wake up the imagination of any gay person. I think Judy Grahn should be compared to Walt Whitman; she is one of our most important contemporary writers.

2. *CHRISTIANITY, SOCIAL TOLERANCE, AND HOMOSEXUALITY: Gay People in Western Europe from the Beginning of the Christian Era to the Fourteenth Century*, by John Boswell

A basic book that every gay person should read.

---

* As a senior editor at St. Martin's Press, Michael Denneny has published more gay and lesbian books over the last decade than any other editor at a commercial company.

3. *LOVE ALONE: Eighteen Elegies for Rog,* by Paul Monette
To my mind this book is simply a classic, one of the most important works to come out of our confrontation with this disastrous AIDS epidemic; this book will be read a hundred years from now.

4. *AND THE BAND PLAYED ON: Politics, People, and the AIDS Epidemic,* by Randy Shilts
A sweeping, epic work — as much a political act that changed how AIDS was seen in this country, as a book. Basic to gay history.

5. *ZAMI: A New Spelling of my Name,* by Audre Lorde
A powerful autobiography by one of the great women of our time; remarkable writing, remarkable life.

6. *THE SWIMMING POOL LIBRARY,* by Alan Hollinghurst
Virtually a history of gay sensibility in England in the twentieth century, as well as a superb novel.

7. *DANCER FROM THE DANCE,* by Andrew Holleran
The novel about gay life in the seventies, it's *The Great Gatsby* of gay life.

8. *NOTES FROM AN AUTOBIOGRAPHY,* by Sam Steward
This story of gay life from the thirties to the seventies is just a joy to read.

9. *RUBYFRUIT JUNGLE,* by Rita Mae Brown
When this book came out — way back when — it was not only exhilarating, it felt like a lifeline when there was little else to hold on to.

10. *ONE LAST WALTZ,* by Ethan Mordden
Mordden's only novel, completely neglected by the critics and the public, is simply a perfect work of art and a wonderful, profound novel.

ARTEMIS OAKGROVE'S
10 FAVORITE LESBIAN BOOKS*

1. *I AM A WOMAN,* by Ann Bannon
Beebo Brinker was my first fiction crush back in 1977.

2. *THE DAY WE WERE MOSTLY BUTTERFLIES,* by Louise B. King
Hysterically funny.

3. *AGAINST THE SEASON,* by Jane Rule
Suave butches are a weakness with me.

4. *PATIENCE AND SARAH,* by Isabel Miller
Gender-confused butches are another weakness.

5. *SAY JESUS AND COME TO ME,* by Ann Allen Shockley
The good reverend can have her way with me anytime.

6. *SEX IN THE SHADOWS,* by Randy Salem
Seducing a prostitute and giving her a virgin's orgasm is perfect.

7. *LIFE AND DEATH OF RADCLYFFE HALL,* by Lady Una Troubridge
Helped me keep it together when I got down on myself as a writer.

8. *THE AMAZON OF LETTERS: The Life and Loves of Natalie Barney,* by George Wickes
Totally romantic lifestyle.

9. *THE COLOR PURPLE,* by Alice Walker
Brilliantly crafted story.

10. *MACHO SLUTS,* by Pat Califia
Hottest stuff I've ever read.

---

* Artemis Oakgrove is the founder of Lace Publications and author of such lesbian erotica as *The Throne Trilogy.*

CARRIE BARNETT'S 10 FAVORITE LESBIAN WORKS OF FICTION*

1. *MURDER AT THE NIGHTWOOD BAR,* by Katherine V. Forrest
Because I *am* Kate Delafield!

2. *A PLACE AT THE TABLE,* by Edith Konecky
Konecky creates a rich texture in this well-written story of a woman's mid-life coming of age.

3. *SHOULDERS,* by Georgia Cottrell
I like Cottrell's writing and her story of coming out is similar to my own.

4. *THE HAUNTED HOUSE,* by Rebecca Brown.
The entire time I was reading this work, I thought I hated it. When I finished it, I cried. It touched me deeply.

5. THE COMPLETE BEEBO BRINKER SERIES, by Ann Bannon
These were my first glimpses into lesbian fiction. They gave me insight into our history and culture.

6. *CURIOUS WINE,* by Katherine V. Forrest
A classic. Maybe *the* classic.

7. *DESERT OF THE HEART,* by Jane Rule
Rule is one of our greatest writers. This book has incredible depth and character.

8. *BEDROCK,* by Lisa Alther
This work, like her others, is rich in character, humor, and insight.

9. *TRAVELS WITH DIANA HUNTER,* by Regine Sands
Ribald, P.I., and wellwritten. To be read aloud in bed.

---

* Carrie Barnett is co-owner of Chicago's People Like Us bookstore.

10. *CITY OF SORCERY,* by Marion Zimmer Bradley
I fantasize about being an alien Amazon on a quest. Perhaps I am.

JESSE MONTEAGUDO'S
10 UNFAVORITE GAY BOOKS*

1. *EVERYTHING YOU ALWAYS WANTED TO KNOW ABOUT SEX (BUT WERE AFRAID TO ASK),* by Dr. David Reuben
This monstrosity kept me in the closet longer than necessary. The chapter on "Male Homosexuality" is a monument to ignorance.

2–10. *THE LORD WON'T MIND, ON FOR THE GODS, FORTH INTO LIGHT, AN IDOL FOR OTHERS, THE QUIRK, NOW LET'S TALK ABOUT MUSIC, PERFECT FREEDOM, THE GREAT URGE DOWNWARD,* and *A MEASURE OF MADNESS,* by Gordon Merrick
Merrick's Harlequin romances are the worst books to ever top gay bestseller lists. His men are stuck in a thirties' time-warp, artisticallly and politically.

JESSE MONTEAGUDO'S
10 FAVORITE GAY BOOKS

1. *ANOTHER MOTHER TONGUE: Gay Words, Gay Worlds,* by Judy Grahn
I always suspected that there was more to being gay than sex. Here Grahn proves it, in prose as rich as poetry.

---

* Jesse Monteagudo is book reviewer for the *Weekly News* in Miami.

2. *THE CELLULOID CLOSET: Homosexuality in the Movies,* by Vito Russo
   This book combines two of my favorite topics, gays and movies. It is also well written.

3. *CHRISTIANITY, SOCIAL TOLERANCE, AND HOMOSEXUALITY: Gay People in Western Europe from the Beginning of the Christian Era to the Fourteenth Century,* by John Boswell
   Boswell's book proves that scholarship and good reading are not mutually exclusive.

4. *FAULTLINE,* by Sheila Ortiz Taylor
   Move over, Rita Mae Brown! Taylor's tale of lesbian motherhood among the rabbits is to gay wit what the San Andreas Fault is to rock formations.

5. *GAY AMERICAN HISTORY,* by Jonathan Katz
   Katz's treasure-trove of relevant documents is a labor of love and an education in itself. Even (especially) the footnotes are worth reading.

6. *A GAY DIARY,* by Donald Vining (in four volumes)
   I have great respect and admiration for the gay men and women who came before us. Like the documents in *Gay American History,* Vining's diaries are an inspiration to us all.

7. *GAY SPIRIT: Myth and Meaning,* by Mark Thompson
   Like Judy Grahn before them, Thompson and his contributors celebrate our people, and chart our special roles in society.

8. *SEX VARIANT WOMEN IN LITERATURE,* by Jeannette H. Foster
   Foster's groundbreaking work is the only pre-Stonewall nonfiction book that can still be read for both pleasure and profit.

9. *SWEET DREAMS: The Mission of Alex Kane #1,* by John Preston
   Preston's superhero novel is the perfect book to give to a young gay boy who's just coming out. If anything, it will make him rush to the nearest gay bookstore to buy the sequels.

10. *TALES OF THE CITY,* by Armistead Maupin
    Along with its five sequels, *Tales of the City* is *the* great American gay novel.

53 GAY AND LESBIAN WRITERS, MAGAZINES, AND PRESSES THAT HAVE RECEIVED NEA GRANTS

Over the last few years, the right of gay and lesbian writers and artists to free expression has come under direct attack from the federal government. As a result of a congressional campaign led by Sen. Jesse Helms (R-N.C.) on the funding policy of the National Endowment of the Arts, all 1990 grant recipients had to agree in writing not to use NEA grant money to produce art that "may be considered obscene ... including but not limited to depictions of sadomasochism, homoeroticism, the sexual exploitation of children, or individuals engaged in sex acts and which, when taken as a whole do not have serious literary, artistic, political or scientific value." What might we lose if the trend continues? Among past grant recipients are:

Writers:

1. PAULA GUNN ALLEN, 1977

2. ROBIN BECKER, 1989

3. FRANK BIDART, 1976, 1985

4. PAUL BOWLES, 1978

5. OLGA BROUMAS, 1977

6. RITA MAE BROWN, 1978

7. KIM CHERNIN, 1990

8. CHRYSTOS, 1990

9. JAN CLAUSEN, 1981

10. MICHELLE CLIFF, 1983, 1989

11. LUCILLE CLIFTON, 1970, 1973

12. ALFRED CORN, 1979

13. MELVIN DIXON, 1984

14. ROBERT DUNCAN, 1967

15. ALLEN GINSBERG, 1979, 1987

16. JUDY GRAHN, 1979

17. SUSAN GRIFFIN, 1976

18. ALLAN GURGANUS, 1976, 1985

19. MARILYN HACKER, 1974, 1985

20. JOY HARJO, 1977

21. ESSEX HEMPHILL, 1986

22. JUNE JORDAN, 1981

23. IRENA KLEPFISZ, 1988

24. JOAN LARKIN, 1987

25. DAVID LEAVITT, 1985

26. AUDRE LORDE, 1981, 1990

27. WILLIAM MEREDITH, 1972

28. JANE MILLER, 1985

29. HONOR MOORE, 1981

30. ROBIN MORGAN, 1979

31. PETER ORLOVSKY, 1979

32. MINNIE BRUCE PRATT, 1990

33. MAY SARTON, 1967

34. JAMES SCHUYLER, 1972

35. MAY SWENSON, 1974

36. JOHN WIENERS, 1986

Magazines and Presses:

37. *CALYX,* 1978–1979, 1983–1988, 1990

38. *CHRYSALIS,* 1979

39. *CONDITIONS,* 1979–1982

40. CROSSING PRESS, 1975–1977, 1979

41. *DARK HORSE,* 1978

42. *FAG RAG,* 1977

43. FEMINIST PRESS, 1975, 1978

44. GAY SUNSHINE PRESS, 1976–1977, 1979–1981, 1984

45. *HELICON NINE,* 1985–1986, 1988

46. KITCHEN TABLE PRESS, 1987

47. MANROOT PRESS, 1975–1976

48. SEAL PRESS, 1977, 1980–1981, 1984–1985, 1987–1988

49. SHAMELESS HUSSY PRESS, 1977, 1980

50. SPINSTERS INK, 1983

51. SPINSTERS/AUNT LUTE, 1988, 1990

52. *13TH MOON,* 1977–1978, 1981–1982

53. VIOLET PRESS, 1975–1976

Daring to

Speak Our Name

8 BUTTON SLOGANS OF THE 1960S

1. EQUALITY FOR HOMOSEXUALS
2. WARNING: SODOMY CAN BE HABIT-FORMING
3. CHASTE MAKES WASTE
4. UNBUTTON
5. PHALLIC SYMBOLS ARISE
6. IF IT MOVES, FONDLE IT
7. BE PECULIAR
8. DOWN WITH PANTS

18 POST-STONEWALL BUTTON SLOGANS

1. BETTER BLATANT THAN LATENT
2. AN ARMY OF LOVERS CANNOT LOSE
3. OUT OF THE CLOSETS AND INTO THE STREETS
4. WE ARE EVERYWHERE
5. A WOMAN WITHOUT A MAN IS LIKE A FISH WITHOUT A BICYCLE
6. MOTHER NATURE IS A LESBIAN
7. LESBIAN VISIBILITY IS LESBIAN SURVIVAL
8. BETTER GAY THAN GRUMPY
9. IT'S A BITCH BEING BUTCH
10. KEEP YOUR LAWS OFF MY BODY
11. BORN-AGAIN LESBIAN

12. THE MORAL MAJORITY IS NEITHER

13. CLOSETS ARE FOR CLOTHES

14. HOW DARE YOU PRESUME I'M HETEROSEXUAL!

15. LESBIANS IGNITE

16. LESBIANS HAVE NATURAL RHYTHM

17. I OWN MY BODY — BUT I SHARE

18. WE ARE ANGRY, NOT GAY

10 ABSURD ARRESTS OF PEOPLE ... AND 1 OF A PSEUDO-PENIS

1. ROSA BONHEUR

Nineteenth-century artist Rosa Bonheur had a special authorization from the French government allowing her to wear men's clothing "for reasons of health." On one of the few occasions when she did dress in the women's fashions of her day, she was arrested for female impersonation.

2. DAVID FOLLETT

Because of his acknowledged gayness in a state which still had anti-sodomy laws, David Follett was denied a driver's license by the state of Connecticut in 1970. Follett had received a temporary license but the commissioner of motor vehicles, John Tynan, refused to grant him a permanent license. Tynan's decision was backed up by the state attorney general, Robert Killian.

Follett was then arrested while driving after his temporary permit had expired. The Connecticut Civil Liberties Union planned to take the case to court, but the issue became moot the following year when Connecticut's anti-sodomy laws were abolished.

3. TOM ECKLER

As Tom Eckler walked down a Los Angeles street wearing his new "Gay Power — Christopher Street West '70" button, a policeman came up next to him and commented, "You're one of those queers, ain't you?" The officer then confiscated the pin. Eckler quipped, "Wear it in good health, dear," upon which the officer handcuffed and frisked him, then arrested him for engaging in lewd conduct with a police officer.

4. RICHARD CHINN and JOHN CANTRELL

Chinn and Cantrell were arrested for disorderly conduct and public indecency when they kissed each other goodbye at a Chicago bus stop in 1971. Bail was set at $1,000 each. The arrests were followed by mass protests during Gay Pride Week a month later, and charges were dropped.

5. CAROL DOWNER

In the "Great Yogurt Conspiracy Trial" of Los Angeles, Carol Downer was acquitted of practicing medicine without a license. The 1973 case resulted from a police raid on the Los Angeles Feminist Women's Health Center's Self-Help Clinic, of which Downer was the founder. The crime? Downer had helped another woman cure a vaginal yeast infection with plain yogurt.

6. AUSTRALIAN SUNBATHERS

A major police operation took place at Lady Jane Beach outside of Sydney, Australia, in 1974. "Plainclothes" officers infiltrated the crowd at the beach, then were joined by two boatloads of an amphibious unit that had been using telescopes to observe the beach from the ocean. The undertaking resulted in arrests of forty-two nude gay and lesbian sunbathers.

7. Z BUDAPEST

Z Budapest was arrested for fortune-telling in 1975 after giving a tarot card reading to an undercover police officer in Los Angeles. Budapest, identified as the lesbian founder of the Susan B. Anthony Coven Number One, explained that the card readings were a genuine part of her religion. The judge meted out a 180-day suspended sentence, two years probation, and a $300 fine.

8. VALLOT MARTINELLI, JEANNE BARNEY, JOHN EMBRY, and DOUGLAS HOLLIDAY

A charity slave auction held by the Los Angeles leather community was raided by police in 1976, with organizers, bidders, and slaves arrested. After intense controversy, the D.A.'s office dropped charges against everyone but the event's four main organizers, who were charged with pandering.

The "slaves" at the auction were all volunteers, helping to raise money for the local Gay Community Services Center. The elaborate staging and costumes were, according to organizer Barney, "all theater." A second auction was held to help pay court costs for the defendants.

9. CARL HILL

British antique dealer Carl Hill was arrested twice under U.S. immigration policies barring admittance of gay men and lesbians. In 1978, he was arrested at the San Francisco International Airport while wearing a gay pride pin. The uproar over his case triggered a policy change, stating that only self-acknowledged lesbians and gay men would be prevented from entering the country.

Unhappy with having achieved only a small change in the homophobic policy, Hill returned to the same airport in 1980. Walking up to a customs official, Hill declared, "I must inform you that I am a homosexual." He was again arrested, but an administrative hearing ruled that the policy was unenforceable.

10. UNIFORM LOVERS

Denver police arrested two gay men at the 1984 American Uniform Association Convention. Both men were wearing uniforms similar to those worn by local cops, an act forbidden by city ordinance. The case was struck down by Judge Irwin Ettenberg, who said the ordinance was unconstitutionally broad.

11. A PENIS?

At the 1971 Christopher Street West parade in Hollywood, police confiscated a parade prop that they thought to be a giant penis, claiming that they wished to examine the item and determine if charges of some sort should be brought against its owners. The item in question was actually a paper Chinese dragon, common in many Asian parades and celebrations.

13 USES OF THE "GAY PANIC" DEFENSE

1. VINCENT WELCH, Florida, 1974

Nineteen-year-old Vincent Welch beat a man to death. He pleaded guilty, but said the victim had lured him to a motel and made sexual advances at him.

A psychologist testifying on Welch's behalf said that Welch "unwittingly was victimized with an abnormal situation, was thrown into a homosexual panic, and acted out a rage reaction. What happened to Vince could very well have happened to any red-blooded, fun-seeking American boy. To ruin this young man's life with a prison sentence would only seem vengeful and inane." Welch was sentenced to probation and told to seek psychiatric treatment.

2. ALFRED SMITH, JR., New Jersey, 1976

Smith confessed to murdering 21-year-old Dorsey Burnett only after a police officer suggested to him that Burnett *looked* gay and told him that under New Jersey law, a murderer could plead self-defense if the victim had made a homosexual advance. Claiming that Burnett had done so, Smith led police to the body.

3. ANDREW TONEY, California, 1982

Toney was acquitted of murder after he claimed that the victim had made sexual advances toward him, throwing him into a rage.

4. MATTHEW WARRING and KEVIN KINNAHAN, Washington, D.C., 1984

These high school seniors approached William Hassell in a gay bar, invited him to a party, then drove him to a local park.

There they forced him to strip at knifepoint, kicked him repeatedly in the groin, threatened to castrate him, and urinated on him.

Warring and Kinnahan pleaded guilty to assault. The judge in the case said he was "satisfied" with their claims that they were drunk and that a "sexual advance" by Hassell had precipitated their attack. He let them off with probation.

5. DAVID PATE, Alabama, 1985

Pate met John Michael Timpa in a bar and visited his apartment several times. They then went for a drive together, and when they stopped to urinate, Pate shot Timpa. He was convicted of the lesser charge of manslaughter, rather than murder, after testifying that Timpa had tried to force him to have sex.

6. TERRY KERR, Michigan, 1986

Kerr claimed to be acting in self-defense after victim Henry Wayne Watson allegedly grabbed at a friend's genitals. According to the friend, Kerr repeatedly kicked Watson — who did not fight back — with steel-toed workboots, "until the blood sprayed from his face"; Kerr then came back with another friend to finish Watson off with a sledgehammer. Kerr bragged to friends before his arrest that he had killed a "fag."

Even though his two accomplices pleaded guilty to related charges, Kerr pleaded not guilty, and a jury acquitted him of all charges.

7. DAVID STEWART, Michigan, 1986

A jury convicted Stewart of second-degree murder despite his claim that he killed Wayne Waltz to avoid being raped by him. The jurors were apparently convinced by the prosecutor's argument that if Stewart truly had felt threatened, he had had time to flee.

8. DEAN LUDWIG BEE, West Virginia, 1986

Bee said in a taped confession that while drinking in a bar he accepted a ride home from F. Dent Hickman, whom he had just met. He fell asleep in the car, then awoke in a "strange house" to find Hickman licking ketchup and mayonnaise off of his nude body. He "went crazy," Bee said, and stabbed Hickman with a knife he grabbed from the nightstand. A jury found Bee not guilty of murder.

9. STEVEN WHITE, Ohio, 1988

According to the testimony of an accomplice, White had intended to burgle the home of a gay man because "a homosexual's not going to report it." He ended up beating and strangling the man to death.

On trial, White claimed to have committed the murder in self-defense after the victim tried to force him to have oral sex. He was found guilty anyway. In sentencing White to the maximum prison sentence permitted by law, Judge Norbert Nadel said, "Justice requires that I place the same value on [the victim's] life as I would on the life of any other unfortunate crime victim, regardless of lifestyle."

10. JOHN MILLER, Minnesota, 1988

Miller claimed that his boss, a gay man who had befriended and hired him, made sexual advances toward him; in response, Miller stabbed him — fifteen times. A jury convicted him of second-degree murder.

11. UNIDENTIFIED TEENAGER, California, 1988

A teenage boy in San Francisco stabbed his gay neighbor to death with a butcher knife, claiming that the man had approached him sexually and had attacked his twelve-year-old sister. Though the youth was convicted of manslaughter, the judge in the case angered local gays when he called the murdered man "reprehensible" and "criminal" — apparently blaming him for his own death.

12. BRIAN DIETRICH, Louisiana, 1988

Dietrich stabbed his gay victim fifteen times, then stole his money and rings. Though Dietrich's attorney argued that the victim had made violent and aggressive sexual advances toward Dietrich, causing him to panic, the prosecutor asserted that

Dietrich had deliberately set out to "roll a queer." The jury convicted Dietrich of murder.

13. MARTY RAY WITHERS, Utah, 1990
    Withers went on a drinking binge and blacked out. When he came to, he testified,he found a semi-nude man tugging at his pants. "I was scared to death, I feared for my life, and I wasn't about to let anybody do any homosexual things to me," Withers said, explaining why he had stabbed the man to death with his pocket knife. A jury acquitted him of murder.

11 BOYCOTTS OF THE PAST AND PRESENT

1. TOWER RECORDS, 1969, for firing an employee from its San Francisco store because he was bisexual

2. *LOS ANGELES TIMES,* 1969, for refusing to allow the word "homosexual" to appear in any advertising

3. MACY'S, 1971, for helping to entrap and prosecute homosexuals engaged in sex in restrooms in its San Francisco store

4. COORS BREWING CO., 1976–ongoing, first for its anti-gay employment practices and anti-gay statements by its owners, and later for its large financial contributions to anti-gay organizations

5. GREYHOUND BUS LINES, 1980, for actively helping right-wing fundamentalists to put together a national rally in Washington, D.C.

6. HOLIDAY INNS, 1980, for harassment of the Southeastern Conference of Lesbians and Gays, held in a Memphis Holiday Inn in August 1979

7. VISA, 1988, for its sponsorship of the U.S. Olympics despite the U.S. Olympic Committee's legal harassment of the Gay Games and its refusal to allow the Gay Games to be called the "Gay Olympics"

Raymond Proulx

Clipped Visa cards were used to make a banner protesting Visa's support of the anti-gay U.S. Olympic Committee. The banner also memorialized Tom Waddell, founder of the Gay Games, who died in 1987 of AIDS-related complications.

8. DONNA SUMMER, 1980s, for homophobic remarks

9. WESTERN UNION, 1990, for attempting to challenge the legality of the San Francisco gay rights ordinance

10. PHILIP MORRIS CO. — MARLBORO CIGARETTES and MILLER BEER, 1990, for Philip Morris's support of Sen. Jesse Helms's campaign for re-election and a $200,000 contribution to the Jesse Helms Citizenship Center, a museum and library being built in Helms's honor that is scheduled to open in 1992

11. SNAP (the music group), 1990, for a gay-bashing incident involving its lead singer at a gay bar in Boston, where Snap had performed as part of an AIDS benefit

13 EVENTS THAT USED THE WORD "OLYMPICS" IN THEIR NAME

1. SPECIAL OLYMPICS

2. BRIDGE OLYMPICS

3. INTERNATIONAL POLICE OLYMPICS

4. RAT OLYMPICS

5. ARMENIAN OLYMPICS

6. K-9 OLYMPICS

7. SENIOR OLYMPICS

8. WHEELCHAIR OLYMPICS

9. ESKIMO OLYMPICS

10. JUNIOR OLYMPICS

11. CRAB COOKING OLYMPICS

12. EXPLORER SCOUT OLYMPICS

13. ARMCHAIR OLYMPICS

In 1987, however, by a 5-to-4 vote, the U.S. Supreme Court ruled in favor of the U.S. Olympic Committee in a lawsuit that forbade the organizers of the Gay Games to use the term *Gay Olympics.*

32 SIGNERS OF A 1975 MS. MAGAZINE PETITION FOR FREEDOM OF SEXUAL CHOICE

1. BELLA ABZUG, *U.S. congresswoman*

2. MAYA ANGELOU, *writer*

3. TI-GRACE ATKINSON, *feminist*

4. CAROL BELLAMY, *N.Y. state senator*

5. RITA MAE BROWN, *writer*

6. CHARLOTTE BUNCH, *editor*

7. PHYLLIS CHESLER, *author*

8. SHIRLEY CHISHOLM, *U.S. congresswoman*

9. KAREN DeCROW, *N.O.W. president*

10. BARBARA DEMING, *writer*

11. FRANCES FITZGERALD, *writer*

12. CAROL GREITZER, *New York City councilwoman*

13. WILMA SCOTT HEIDE, *former N.O.W. president*

14. ELIZABETH HOLTZMAN, *U.S. congresswoman*

15. JILL JOHNSTON, *writer*

16. ERICA JONG, *writer*

17. FLORYNCE KENNEDY, *attorney*

18. JILL KREMENTZ, *photographer*

19. PATRICIA LOUD, *author*

20. MARGARET MEAD, *anthropologist*

21. HELEN S. MEYNER, *U.S. congresswoman*

22. KATE MILLETT, *writer*

23. ANAIS NIN, *writer*

24. JOYCE CAROL OATES, *writer*

25. YOKO ONO, *artist*

26. GAIL THAIN PARKER, *president, Bennington College*

27. ELEANOR PERRY, *film writer and producer*

28. MARGE PIERCY, *poet and novelist*

29. HELEN REDDY, *singer*

30. MALVINA REYNOLDS, *songwriter*

31. LILY TOMLIN, *actress*

32. JOANNE WOODWARD, *actress*

16 U.S. SENATORS WHO INTERVENED ON BEHALF OF OPENLY GAY AIR FORCE SGT. LEONARD MATLOVICH IN 1975

1. BIRCH BAYH (D-IN)

2. EDWARD BROOKE (R-MA)

3. JAMES BUCKLEY (R-NY)

4. ALAN CRANSTON (D-CA)

5. MIKE GRAVEL (D-AL)

6. PHILIP HART (D-MI)

7. DANIEL INOUYE (D-HI)

8. EDWARD KENNEDY (D-MA)

9. CHARLES MATHIAS (R-MD)

10. EDMUND MUSKIE (D-ME)

11. CHARLES PERCY (R-IL)

12. ADLAI STEVENSON (D-IL)

13. JOHN TOWER (R-TX)

14. JOHN TUNNEY (D-CA)

15. LOWELL WEICKER (R-CT)

16. HARRISON WILLIAMS (D-NJ)

18 PRO-GAY REPUBLICANS

1. Sen. JOHN TOWER (Tex.)

In 1976, Purple-Heart recipient Leonard Matlovich came out and was discharged from the Air Force. Tower, not known for being progressive, angrily reacted with a pro-gay statement. He expressed support for gay rights legislation on other occasions, as well.

2. Rep. PETE McCLOSKEY (Calif.)

Liberal on many issues, McCloskey was at one time the only Republican co-sponsor of the federal gay rights bill.

3. Sen. JIM JEFFORDS (Vt.)

Jeffords was a strong supporter of gay rights legislation while in the U.S. House, and shows every sign of continuing now that he's in the Senate.

4. Rep. JOEL PRITCHARD (Wash.)

As early as 1976, Pritchard supported gay rights legislation.

5. Sen. EDWARD BROOKE (Mass.)

Brooke, the first black member of the U.S. Senate in this century, was a strong and articulate supporter of civil rights for gay people.

6. Gov. JAY S. HAMMOND (Alaska)

In 1976, Gov. Hammond instructed his state's Equal Employment Opportunity Commission to look into ways to stop anti-gay discrimination.

Rep. Pete McCloskey of California (left) and Sen. Jim Jeffords of Vermont are strong supporters of gay rights, despite their party's continuing anti-gay bias.

7. State Sen. ROBERT A. HALL (Mass.)

In 1972, Hall won office in a heavily Democratic and very Catholic district by a margin of only 126 votes. Observers called him a lunatic when he became a champion of a gay rights bill, and his 1974 opponent tried to use it against him. But Hall responded in newspaper ads that he didn't think the state should have to raise taxes just to support gay people on welfare simply because some employers wouldn't hire them. He won re-election by a landslide. Perhaps Hall knew something: A decade later, the town clerk of Lunenberg, his small home town, became the country's first elected Republican official to come out.

8. State Rep. WILLIAM G. ROBINSON (Mass.)

The Republican party in Massachusetts has long been a minority, yet often a majority of Republicans have supported a gay rights issue in the statehouse, while Democrats have prevented passage. In 1975, when a Democratic legislator was haranguing against "dykes and queers," Assistant House Minority Leader William Robinson asked to have him removed from the chamber.

9. Sen. LOWELL WEICKER (Conn.)

An outspoken advocate of gay rights and funding for AIDS treatment programs, including an AZT distribution program, Weicker was one of only two Republican senators to cosponsor a 1988 gay and lesbian civil rights bill.

10. Sen. JOHN CHAFEE (R.I.)

He was the other Republican cosponsor of the 1988 civil rights bill.

11. Rep. STEWART McKINNEY (Conn.)

McKinney was long an outspoken supporter of gays with regard to AIDS programs and civil rights issues, as well as a staunch advocate for the homelesss. Only after his AIDS-related death in 1987 did it become widely known that he himself, although married, also had a gay lover.

12. Mayor ROGER HEDGECOCK (Calif.)

Though both Hedgecock and his Democratic opponent in the 1983 run-off election for mayor of San Diego had support from gays, Hedgecock, a moderate Republican, was perceived as more sensitive to gay concerns, and won the election.

13–16. Rep. BILL GREEN (N.Y.), Rep. CONNIE MORELLA (Md.), Rep. JOHN MILLER (Wash.), and Rep. CHRISTOPHER SHAYS (Conn.)

Cosponsors of a 1988 anti-discrimination bill in the House.

17. State Rep. JAMES DRESSEL (Mich.)

In 1983 Dressel proposed a comprehensive bill to ban anti-gay discrimination in education, employment, housing, and public accommodations throughout Michigan.

18. D.A. GARY FLAKNE (Minn.)

Elected county prosecuting attorney for Minneapolis in the

mid-seventies, Flakne had a long record of supporting gay rights in his previous role as a state representative.

15 TOP SENATORS*

1. ADAMS (D-WA)

2. BRADLEY (D-NJ)

3. BURDICK (D-ND)

4. CHAFEE (R-RI)

5. CRANSTON (D-CA)

6. DOMENICI (R-NM)

7. INOUYE (D-HI)

8. JEFFORDS (R-VT)

9. KENNEDY (D-MA)

10. LEAHY (D-VT)

11. MATSUNAGA (D-HI)

12. MIKULSKI (D-MD)

13. MOYNIHAN (D-NY)

14. PELL (D-RI)

15. SIMON (D-IL)

---

* These lists are based on evaluations of voting records, compiled by the National Gay and Lesbian Task Force.

...AND 93 TOP MEMBERS OF THE U.S. HOUSE OF REPRESENTATIVES

1. ACKERMAN (D-NY)

2. BEILENSON (D-CA)

3. BERMAN (D-CA)

4. BONIOR (D-MI)

5. BOXER (D-CA)

6. BROWN (D-CA)

7. BUSTAMANTE (D-TX)

8. CARDIN (D-MD)

9. CLAY (D-MO)

10. COLLINS (D-IL)

11. CONYERS (D-MI)

12. COYNE (D-PA)

13. DELLUMS (D-CA)

14. DIXON (D-CA)

15. DOWNEY (D-NY)

16. DYMALLY (D-CA)

17. EARLY (D-MA)

18. EDWARDS (D-CA)

19. ENGEL (D-NY)

20. FASCELL (D-FL)

21. FAZIO (D-CA)

22. FEIGHAN (D-OH)

23. FLAKE (D-NY)

24. FOGLIETTA (D-PA)

25. FORD (D-MI)

26. FRANK (D-MA)

27. FROST (D-TX)

28. GARCIA (D-NY)

29. GEJDENSON (D-CT)

30. GEPHARDT (D-MO)

31. GONZALES (D-TX)

32. GRADISON (R-OH)

33. GREEN (D-NY)

34. HAWKINS (D-CA)

35. HAYS (D-IL)

36. HOYER (D-MD)

37. JOHNSTON (D-FL)

38. KASTENMEIER (D-WI)

39. KENNEDY (D-MA)

40. KOSTMAYER (D-PA)

41. LEHMAN (D-FL)

42. LEVIN (D-MI)

43. LEVINE (D-CA)

44. LEWIS (D-GA)

45. LOWEY (D-NY)

46. MANTON (D-NY)

47. MARKEY (D-MA)

48. MARTINEZ (D-CA)

49. MATSUI (D-CA)

50. MAZZOLI (D-KY)

51. MCDERMOTT (D-WA)

52. MCHUGH (D-NY)

53. MFUME (D-MD)

54. MILLER (D-CA)

55. MINETA (D-CA)

56. MOODY (D-WI)

57. MORELLA (R-MD)

58. MORRISON (D-CT)

59. MRAZEK (D-NY)

60. NAGLE (D-IA)

61. OAKAR (D-OH)

62. OBERSTAR (D-MN)

63. OLIN (D-VA)

64. OWENS (D-NY)

65. PANETTA (D-CA)

66. PAYNE (D-NJ)

67. PEASE (D-OH)

68. PELOSI (D-CA)

69. ROYBAL (D-CA)

70. SABO (D-MN)

71. SAVAGE (D-IL)

72. SCHEUER (D-NY)

73. SCHNEIDER (R-RI)

74. SCHROEDER (D-CO)

75. SCHUMER (D-NY)

76. SIKORSKI (D-MN)

77. SOLARZ (D-NY)

78. STARK (D-CA)

79. STOKES (D-OH)

80. STUDDS (D-MA)

81. SWIFT (D-WA)

82. TORRES (D-CA)

83. TOWNS (D-NY)

84. UNSOELD (D-WA)

85. VENTO (D-MN)

86. VISCLOSKY (D-IN)

87. WAXMAN (D-CA)

88. WEISS (D-NY)

89. WHEAT (D-MO-5)

90. WILLIAMS (D-MT)

91. WOLPE (D-MI)

92. WYDEN (D-OR)

93. YATES (D-IL)

11 NATIONAL UNIONS THAT HAVE SUPPORTED GAY RIGHTS

1. AFL-CIO

2. AMERICAN FEDERATION OF STATE, COUNTY, AND MUNICIPAL EMPLOYEES

3. AMERICAN FEDERATION OF TEACHERS

4. AMERICAN POSTAL WORKERS UNION

5. INTERNATIONAL LONGSHOREMEN'S AND WAREHOUSEMEN'S UNION

6. NATIONAL EDUCATION ASSOCIATION

7. OFFICE AND PROFESSIONAL EMPLOYEES INTERNATIONAL UNION

8. SCREEN ACTORS GUILD

9. SERVICE EMPLOYEES INTERNATIONAL UNION

10. UNITED AUTO AND AEROSPACE WORKERS UNION

11. UNITED ELECTRICAL, RADIO AND MACHINE WORKERS OF AMERICA

13 SUCCESSFUL LAWSUITS

1. GARY VAN OOTEGHEM: Awarded $56,000 in back pay, plus reinstatement. Van Ooteghem had been fired from his county job in 1975 because of his advocacy of gay civil rights. The county appealed the case all the way to the Supreme Court, but lost.

2. THOMAS WOOD: Awarded $7,500 when police, without just cause, raided and closed his gay bar two days before the 1982

Mardi Gras festival started in New Orleans.

3. RUTH GRAY: Awarded $5,000 under a District of Columbia anti-discrimination statute when a ballroom refused to rent her space for a gay dance.

4. LEONARD MATLOVICH: Won $160,000 in an out-of-court settlement with the U.S. Air Force after he had been discharged for being gay.

5. PAUL CRONAN: Awarded $1.5 million for discrimination and breach of privacy in 1986, after the New England Telephone Company told other workers he had AIDS, then fired him.

6. DON McGUIRE: Awarded $111,000 in 1987 from city officials in Garden Grove, California, after police harassment forced him to close his gay bar in that city.

7. THE DICK KRAMER GAY MEN'S CHORALE: Awarded $2250 from Archbishop John Quinn of San Francisco. The archbishop had cancelled the group's use of St. Boniface Church four days before a scheduled performance in 1985, merely because the word *gay* appeared in the group's name.

8. KILLIAN SWIFT: Successfully settled out of court (details were not disclosed) in 1987, after initiating a lawsuit against the Reagan White House. Swift claimed he had lost his job as a transcriber in 1984 after the White House had revoked his security pass because he was gay. The White House admitted that it had improperly discriminated against him.

9. JERRY SLOAN: Awarded $8982.20 from Jerry Falwell. In an apparent effort to tone down his image, Falwell denied that he had once called the Metropolitan Community Church "a vile and satanic system." Sloan challenged the denial, and Falwell publicly offered to pay him $5,000 if Sloan could prove his claim. Sloan returned with videotapes of Falwell's original statement. Falwell tried to renege, but a court order forced him to pay — by which

time interest payments and court costs had nearly doubled the amount.

10. KAREN ULANE: Awarded about $130,000 in back pay from Eastern Airlines after she was fired in 1981 following a sex-change operation. The judge ruled that transsexuals were covered by civil rights laws.

11. DARRELL DOWNEY: Awarded $57,000 in 1986 after superiors at work played back for co-workers a phone conversation revealing that Downey was gay.

12. RICKY, RANDY, AND ROBERT RAY: Settled out of court for about $500,000, plus a similar amount in costs, after school authorities barred them from attending classes in Arcadia, Florida, because the boys had been exposed to AIDS.

13. GLORIA ALLRED: Awarded $20,000 and a written apology from California state senator John Schmitz after he called her "a slick butch lawyeress."

MAKING OUR WAY

9 PRO AND CON COMMENTS ABOUT OUTING

1. "Outing is nothing less than psychological rape."
   —*Dave Pallone, former major league baseball umpire,*
   quoted in Edge magazine, 1990

2. "One of the most common charges against outing (and ACT UP) is that both 'go too far'; that they cross some accepted social and political boundary. But the gay movement — and any political movement — has always had to continually 'go too far' in order to get ahead. Certainly the queens, drags, dykes and street queers on Christopher Street went too far when they declared open war on the police at the Stonewall Inn."
   —*Michael Bronski, activist and writer,*
   in The Lavender Network, 1990

3. "I totally disapprove of it. I make an analogy to Jewish law. The Nazi's are coming and I'm a Jew. They know that. You're a Jew. They don't know that. And you're a collaborator. If I kill you myself, the killing is justified as self-defense. If I turn you in for them to tear you limb from limb, the killing is not justified and your blood is on my hands."
   —*Roberta Achtenberg, lesbian activist,*
   quoted in Bay Area Reporter, 1990

4. "If you have agreed to come into [public view], then you have traded most — not all, but most — of your privacy rights."
   —*Gabriel Rotello, editor-in-chief of Outweek magazine,*
   quoted in the Washington Blade

5. "The right to privacy, self-determination, and self-definition are basic feminist principles which exclude 'outing' as a feasible or acceptable strategy to achieve our common goals of equality and liberty." —*Resolution passed by the National*
   Organization for Women, 1990

6. "There have been a lot of people this evening maundering on about our being a powerless minority. Well, when a powerless minority gets a weapon, it uses it — and uses it physically! If you call that blackmail, it is and it should be!"
—Longtime gay activist Frank Kameny,
at a forum on outing

7. "The government has claimed that there is no constitutional right to privacy. I think it is wrong for us to argue that the government grant us the control to make our own sexual choices when we are unwilling to allow others to exercise that same right." *—Urvashi Vaid, executive director of the*
National Lesbian and Gay Task Force,
at the same forum as Kameny;
both quoted in the Washington Blade

8. "I'm outraged by the hypocrisy of the mainstream press when it criticizes outing. Almost every newspaper in the country does it — from the *New York Times* to the *Boston Globe* and most recently the student-run *Harvard Crimson*. These papers have consistently printed names and addresses of men who were arrested for sexual-related activities. That's certainly a form of outing." *—Kevin Cathcart, executive director of*
Gay and Lesbian Advocates and Defenders, 1990

9. "Instead of 'outing' celebrities, I think we should just stop dating them." *—A character drawn by cartoonist Donelan,*
in The Advocate, 1990

Members of ACT UP/Portland outed Sen. Mark Hatfield of Oregon by altering this campaign billboard. They did so to expose Hatfield's hypocrisy in voting anti-gay even though he himself is gay.

9 PEOPLE WHO HAVE BEEN OUTED*

1. RICHARD CHAMBERLAIN, *actor*

2. TAYLOR DAYNE, *singer*

3. MALCOLM FORBES, *multimillionaire publisher*

4. MARK HATFIELD, *Oregon senator*

5. WHITNEY HOUSTON, *singer*

6. KRISTY McNICHOL, *actress*

7. EVELYN MURPHY, *Massachusetts lieutenant governor*

---

* Out of respect for individual privacy, this list includes only those people whose outing has been widely reported. This does not in any way prove that they are gay.

8. JIM THOMPSON, *Illinois governor*

9. JOHN TRAVOLTA, *actor*

7 PORN STARS WHO DIED OF AIDS, AND SOME OF THEIR FILMS

1. KEN J. SAVOIE
   Top Man, Cruisin', The Big One.

2. JOHNNY DAWES (real name: Brian Lee)
   Bad, Bad Boys, Big Business, Hard Line, In the End Zone, Dude Ranch.

3. JOHN HOLMES
   The Biggest of Them All, Too Hard to Handle, A Problem of Size, Sex Machine, Single Handed.

4. CASEY DONOVAN (real name: Calvin Culver)
   The Boys in the Sand, The Other Side of Aspen, Casey, Heatstroke.

5. J.W. KING
   Face to Face, Raw Hide, Big Men on Campus, California Boys, Hot Shots vol. 3–9.

6. KURT MARSHALL
   The Other Side of Aspen II, Night Flight, Sizing Up, Splash Shots.

7. TONY BRAVO (real name: Michael Pietri)
   Boystown, Discharged, The Other Side of Aspen II, Powertool.

10 TOP ATHLETES

1. WILLIAM "BIG BILL" TILDEN

In the 1920s, Tilden dominated tennis as no one had ever dominated any sport. But in 1946 he was arrested for having sex with a minor, and his life fell apart. Yet even in 1949, an Associated Press poll named him the top athlete of the first half of the century, with ten times the votes of the nearest runner-up.

2. SUSAN McGRIEVY

She was a member of the U.S. Olympic team in the 1956 and 1960 games; she's now a prominent attorney and lesbian activist.

3. TOM WADDELL

Founder of the Gay Games, he was first a member of the 1968 U.S. Olympic decathlon team, placing sixth at Mexico City. In 1986 he won a gold medal at the Gay Games for throwing the javelin. He died a year later of an AIDS-related disease.

4. DAVID KOPAY

A pro running back for ten years, Kopay played for the San Francisco Forty-Niners, the Detroit Lions, the Washington Redskins, the New Orleans Saints, and the Green Bay Packers. He came out in 1975 — the first professional athlete in any sport to do so.

5. GLENN BURKE

When he started playing for the L.A. Dogers in 1976, many thought the young baseball player was destined for stardom. But word of his gayness gradually got around, and created severe pressures from the management. He left professional sports four years later.

6. BILLIE JEAN KING

Tennis great Billie Jean King acknowledged in 1981 that she had been lovers with her "secretary," Marilyn Barnett, during the 1970s, calling the relationship a mistake. The relationship came to light when Barnett sued King, claiming that King had promised her lifetime support and a Malibu beach house for taking over management of their household so that King could focus on tennis.

7. CAT CHASE
She was the 1983 ADFPA (American Drug Free Powerlifting Association) national women's champion in her weight class. With Connie Meredith, Chase also started a gay gym in Boston.

8. MARTINA NAVRATILOVA
The Czech-born tennis star, and former head of the Women's Tennis Association, identifies herself as bisexual. Her most talked-about relationship was with novelist Rita Mae Brown.

9 & 10. BOB PARIS and ROD JACKSON
These two bodybuilders married each other in a July 1989 wedding ceremony. That same month, Paris, who won the Mr. Universe and Mr. America titles in 1983, came out publicly in *Ironman* magazine.

2 GAY ARTISTS WHOSE WORK CAUSED A FUSS AT THE CORCORAN GALLERY

1. PAUL CADMUS
In 1934, Paul Cadmus was a young and little-known artist with a distinctive style of painting. Then the Corcoran Art Gallery planned an exhibition of paintings done for the Depression-era Public Works of Art Project. Cadmus's *The Fleet's In!* — a street scene of sailors consorting with prostitutes — was scheduled for inclusion.

Before the show opened, however, a retired admiral saw the painting and demanded its removal from the gallery. The secretary of the Navy joined in, complaining that the scene "evidently originated in the sordid, depraved imagination of

"Disgraceful, sordid, disreputable ... an unwarranted insult" — these were some of the terms used in 1934 to describe Paul Cadmus's scandalous painting "The Fleet's In!"

someone who has no conception of actual conditions in our service."

The painting was removed, and the controversy made headlines. Cadmus was labeled an enfant terrible of the art world, and his career took off.

2. ROBERT MAPPLETHORPE

In 1989, Robert Mapplethorpe was only beginning to establish his reputation as a masterful photographer. Then the Corcoran Art Gallery planned a retrospective exhibition of his work. The show had already been well received at New York's Whitney Museum of American Art.

But in Washington, right-wing politicians led by Sen. Jesse Helms seized the exhibit as an opportunity for demagoguery. In the ensuing furor, the Corcoran canceled the exhibit, then was so severely criticized for that decision that its director resigned. Robert Mapplethorpe became a household name.

4 GAY CARTOON AND COMIC CHARACTERS

1. NORTHSTAR
Comicdom's first gay superhero, Northstar, appeared in 1980, though only gradually was it made clear to readers that he was gay.

2. ANDY LIPPINCOTT
The *Doonesbury* character, drawn by Gary Trudeau, came out way back in 1976.

3. AKBAR and JEFF
The fezzed "Life in Hell" comic strip twins are quite cheerfully gay.

4. HOMER SIMPSON'S SECRETARY
Matt Groening, who has already given us Akbar and Jeff, gave Homer Simpson a gay male secretary in the second season of Groening's hit television show *The Simpsons*. The sultry voice of Karl was provided by Harvey Fierstein.

...AND 5 WE WONDER ABOUT

1. SCHROEDER
The shy and talented *Peanuts* character would far rather play his piano than play baseball or return Lucy's flirts. Sound familiar?

2. BUGS BUNNY
Although decidedly male, Bugs repeatedly found reasons to dress in female garb in many of his cartoons.

3. BATMAN and ROBIN
The idea of Bruce Ward and his handsome young protégé living together in that big mansion raised so many eyebrows that

when *Batman* was filmed in 1989, the producers dropped Robin's character altogether.

4. WONDER WOMAN
   Is there a more quintessential Amazon warrior? *Wonder Woman* comics have also addressed gay issues very directly.

5. CONAN THE BARBARIAN
   Was it really necessary for him to run around in such a skimpy loincloth? Perhaps — after all, he was created by a gay man.

MICHAEL MUSTO'S 5 BEST PARTIES*

1. DIANA ROSS'S PARTY ON THE *INTREPID,* 1984. Diana came up to me and said, "Hi, I'm Diana Ross." I said, "I know," and I almost fainted.

2. LUST PARTY AT THE WORLD, 1988. A photo shoot of nude male models turned into the orgy of the century.

3. STRAIGHT-TO-HELL PARTY AT THE TUNNEL, 1988. As a judge of the best buns contest, I got endless free gropes.

4. CHIP DUCKETT'S BIRTHDAY AT THE ADONIS THEATER, 1989. Porn star Chris Burns got a big hand for taking Jake Corbin's fist (safely gloved, of course) up the butt.

5. JUNE ALLYSON AND ANN MILLER'S 1990 APPEARANCE AT BLOCKBUSTER VIDEO. June wouldn't talk about Depend diapers though she would gladly discuss *Two Sailors and a Girl.*

---

* Michael Musto is a columnist for *The Village Voice.*

ROBERT PATRICK'S
10 FAVORITE GAY PLAYS*

1. *STREET THEATRE,* by Doric Wilson
   A recreation of the glorious and tawdry origins of Gay Life by a pioneer gay playwright who was *there* at the Stonewall Riots.

2. *DEATHTRAP,* by Ira Levin
   An expert play in which the main characters' homosexuality is *not* saved for a shocking ending, but is up-front all along.

3. *GOODNIGHT, I LOVE YOU,* by William M. Hoffman
   A love story of how a fag-hag keeps her fairy-friend's attention.

4. *TORCH SONG TRILOGY,* by Harvey Fierstein
   Three brilliant plays, all the more surprising because they were written to get their author attention as an actor, not as a writer.

5. *BUTLEY,* by Simon Gray
   A bisexual attempting to have his cock and eat it, too, loses everything but his wit.

6. *THE RUFFIAN ON THE STAIRS,* by Joe Orton
   A grief-stricken boy forces the murderer of his lover to kill him, too.

7. *BEER AND RHUBARB PIE,* by Dan Curzon
   The hottest coming-out play.

---

* Robert Patrick's plays have won wide acclaim in both the gay and mainstream media. His works include *T-Shirts, Blue is for Boys,* and *Kennedy's Children.*

8. *SLUTS*, by Ross MacLean
   L.A.'s pioneer gay playwright throws Santa Monica Boulevard hangabouts into a whirlpool of guilt and instant religion.

9. *THE TRUTH IS BAD ENOUGH*, by Michael Kearns
   In a one-man show, Kearns recreates a success-maddened American youth whose obsession led to national media-fraud when he posed as "The Happy Hustler."

10. *BAR DYKES*, by Merrill Harris
   A meticulous recreation of an evening in a 1950s lesbian bar.

KENNEDY SMITH'S
10 BEST LESBIAN ALBUMS

In the *Washington Blade*, writer and critic Kennedy Smith surveyed the state of lesbian music. Her favorites, starting with the best:

1. *I KNOW YOU KNOW*, by Meg Christian (Olivia Records, 1974).

2. *ANNIVERSARY: Meg/Cris at Carnegie Hall*, by Meg Christian and Cris Williamson (Olivia Records, 1983).

3. *THE WAYS A WOMAN CAN BE*, by Teresa Trull (Olivia Records, 1977).

4. *TURNING IT OVER*, by Meg Christian (Olivia Records, 1981).

5. *JADE AND SARSAPARILLA*, by Janet Hood and Linda Langford (Submaureen Records, 1976).

6. *LAVENDER JANE LOVES WOMEN*, by Alix Dobkin, Kay Gardner, and Patches Attom (Women's Wax Work, 1974).

7. *LET IT BE KNOWN*, by Teresa Trull (Olivia Records, 1980).

8. *IMAGINE MY SURPRISE*, by Holly Near (Redwood Records, 1978).

9. *THE CHANGER AND THE CHANGED,* by Cris Williamson (Olivia Records, 1975).

10. *SONGWRITER,* by Margie Adam (Pleiades Records, 1976).

5 PLANNED GAY COMMUNITIES THAT NEVER HAPPENED

1. NORTHERN GERMANY

The first known effort to develop a gay community appears to have taken place in Germany in the early 1920s. A man named Ernst Klopfleisch sought to develop a gay resort in the Harz Mountains but was forced by local authorities to abandon the project. Shortly afterward, he immigrated to the United States, changed his name to Ernest F. Elmhurst, and tried, again unsuccessfully, to start what would have been the second American homosexual organization.

2. ALPINE COUNTY, CALIFORNIA

Alpine County, a sparsely populated county in the Sierra Nevadas on the California–Nevada border, had fewer than 400 registered voters in 1970. So when Don Jackson, at a Gay Liberation Front symposium in San Francisco, proposed that several hundred gays move there and take over the local government to establish a "gay refuge," the idea seemed downright feasible. By summer, groups had formed within the GLF in both the Bay Area and Los Angeles to plan the exodus, and by fall, nearly 500 people had signed up to make the move. But that October word of the project leaked to the mainstream press and Alpine's residents, resentful of the planned "invasion," took action to block it. They finally succeeded, by freezing all real estate sales and adopting an extremely strict building code that would have doubled building costs.

3. "MT. LOVE" (BANKHEAD SPRINGS), CALIFORNIA

A second attempt to establish a gay town fizzled for lack of funds. In early 1971, a lesbian named Pat Love found a deserted mountain resort, owned entirely by an elderly couple, for sale in southern California. Keeping the town's real name secret to avoid some of the problems associated with the Alpine project, she set up an exclusively gay corporation under the name Mt. Love to raise money for the purchase price — $239,000. But though many expressed interest in buying in once the town was a reality, not enough were willing to risk the initial investment, and the effort evaporated.

4. SOMEWHERE IN DIXIE...

In late 1971, gays in the Detroit area, including some members of ONE, formed a group calling itself Town Council to plan a gay colony somewhere in the South. Their aim was to develop a long-range, step-by-step plan to establish a gay community within an already existing, active mainstream community, rather than an exclusively gay one. It never came about.

5. RHYOLITE, NEVADA

Fred Schoonmaker began trying in 1984 to realize his dream of "an exclusive gay destination resort." He planned a 116-acre resort set in Silver Springs, Nevada, with a hotel, casino, golf course, tennis courts, swimming pools, an air strip, and a price tag of $40 million. When investors failed to respond to his fundraising efforts, Schoonmaker tried something new: In 1986, he attempted to buy the ghost town of Rhyolite, Nevada, but again couldn't come up with the money. At last word, he had put down a deposit on a 41-acre goat ranch near the town of Winnemucca in Pershing County, Nevada.

5 AREAS OF THE COUNTRY MOST LIKELY TO PRODUCE WHITE MEN WHO ARE OPEN TO AN INTERRACIAL RELATIONSHIP*

1. THE NORTH MIDWEST (Wisconsin, Minnesota, Iowa, and Michigan)

2. PENNSYLVANIA DUTCH COUNTRY

3. CALIFORNIA

4. THE NEW YORK CITY AREA

5. TEXAS

9 COLORS HISTORICALLY ASSOCIATED WITH HOMOSEXUALITY

1. SCARLET (Imperial Rome)

2. VIOLET (Imperial Rome)

3. GREEN (Imperial Rome, Victorian England, America in the 1930s through 1950s)

4. YELLOW (Victorian England)

5. RED (late nineteenth-century America; male prostitutes wore red ties)

6. PINK (Nazi Germany)

---

* This list appeared in a 1976 *Advocate* article by John Victor Soares, who wrote that "you may be skeptical about this list, but be apprised that many black people have confirmed it."

7. BLUE (present-day Russia)

8. LAVENDER (throughout history and in modern America)

9. RAINBOW (present-day America)

THE 21 MOST COMMON NAMES FOR WOMEN'S BARS

1. Rumors, Rumours

2. Backstreet, Back Street

3. Faces

4. Connection

5. The Rage

6. Tracks, Trax, Traxx

7. Annex

8. Fantasy, Fantasies

9. Paradise

10. Partners

11. Blue Moon

12. Buddy's

13. Different Strokes

14. Flamingo

15. Garbo's

16. Hideaway

17. The Loft

18. Our Place

19. Scandals
20. Sneakers
21. Underground

THE 20 MOST COMMON NAMES FOR GAY MEN'S BARS

1. Backstreet, Back Street
2. Rumors, Rumours
3. Tracks, Traxx, Trax
4. The Brass Rail
5. Buddies, Buddy's
6. Hideaway
7. Paradise
8. The Eagle
9. The Phoenix
10. Chaps
11. Christopher's
12. Faces
13. Fantasies, Fantasy
14. Fraternity House
15. The Loft
16. Numbers
17. Ramrod
18. Rawhide

19. Silver Fox

20. Visions

26 FIRST NAMES ASSOCIATED WITH GAY MEN

1. ABIGAIL (U.S.; a conservative, middle-aged gay)

2. ADELAIDA (Portugese)

3. AGNES (U.S.)

4. ANGIE (U.S)

5. BETTY (U.S.)

6. BILL (U.S.; a masculine gay man)

7. BRUCE (U.S.)

8. CAMILLE (U.S.)

9. CISSY (or SISSY)

10. DETLEV (Germany)

11. EMILE (French)

12. FRANCESCA, or "CHECCA" (Italian)

13. GUSSIE (Australian)

14. JEANETTE, or JANET (Belgium)

15. JESSIE (British)

16. MARGERY

17. MARÍA (Spanish)

18. MARY or MARY ANN (British, U.S.)

19. MOLLY (British)

20. NANCE, or NANCY (British, especially after WWI)

21. NELLIE

22. NOLA

23. PANSY

24. SEYMOUR (U.S.)

25. TOMMY (British)

26. WANDA (U.S.; as in "Wanda Wandwaver")

6 MEN'S FIRST NAMES USED BY PROMINENT WOMEN

1. JOHN
   Radclyffe Hall believed that her lesbianism represented an "inversion" — that she was a man trapped in a woman's body. This theme comes through strongly in her novel *The Well of Loneliness,* and is one reason the book seems so dated today. For much of her life, Hall called herself John.

2 & 3. MICHAEL and HENRY
   Poets Katherine Harris Bradley (Michael) and Edith Emma Cooper (Henry) lived together, slept together, and wrote poetry and plays together. They called each other by these male names, and published their joint works as "Michael Field."

4. WILLIAM
   From the ages of fourteen to eighteen, poet Willa Cather strongly identified as a male. She got a crew cut, dressed in men's clothes, and called herself William Cather, Jr.

5. GEORGE
   Dr. S. Josephine Baker, famous for identifying "Typhoid

Would you believe "William" Cather?

Mary," used the name George; the memoirs of her lover, I.A.R. Wylie, were titled *My Life with George*.

6. GEORGE, again

Amandine Aurore Lucie Dupin wrote under the name George Sand. She had love affairs with both men and women.

28 QUILT NAMES

1. MICHAEL BENNETT, *director/choreographer*

2. MEL BOOZER, *black- and gay-rights activist*

3. ARTHUR BRESSAN, Jr., *filmmaker*

4. ROY COHN, *attorney*

5. PERRY ELLIS, *fashion designer*

6. DAN EICHOLTZ, *cartoonist*

7. WAYLAND FLOWERS, *comedian*

8. MICHEL FOUCAULT, *philosopher*

9. PHILIP-DIMITRI GALAS, *playwright*

10. KEITH HARING, *artist*

11. ROCK HUDSON, *actor*

12. LIBERACE, *performer*

13. CHARLES LUDLUM, *actor/director/playwright*

14. ROBERT MAPPLETHORPE, *artist/photographer*

15. LEONARD MATLOVICH, *gay-rights activist*

16. STEWART McKINNEY, *U.S. Congressman (R-Conn.)*

17. COURT MILLER, *actor*

18. ED MOCK, *choreographer*

19. KLAUS NOMI, *performance artist*

20. MAX ROBINSON, *ABC News anchor*

21. JERRY SMITH, *Washington Redskin*

22. WILLI SMITH, *fashion designer*

23. CHRISTOPHER STRYKER, *actor*

24. STEPHEN STUCKER, *actor*

25. SYLVESTER, *singer*

26. Dr. TOM WADDELL, *Olympic athlete*

27. RYAN WHITE, *activist*

28. RICKY WILSON, *guitarist with the B-52s*

78 MATERIALS USED IN MAKING QUILT PANELS

1. AFGHANS

2. ARTIFICIAL FLOWERS

3. BABY CLOTHES

4. BALLET SLIPPERS

5. BANDANAS

6. BARBIE DOLLS

7. BASEBALL CAPS

8. BEDSPREAD

9. BRIEFCASE

10. BURLAP

11. BUS TICKETS

12. BUTTONS

13. CARPET

14. CHEF'S HAT

15. COOKING UTENSILS

16. CORDUROY

17. CORSETS

18. CREDIT CARDS

19. CREMATION ASHES

20. CURTAINS

21. DOLL CLOTHES

22. DOLL FURNITURE

23. DRESSES

24. DRIVER'S LICENSES

25. FEATHER BOAS

26. FIRST-PLACE RIBBONS

27. FISHNET HOSE

28. FLAGS

29. FLANNEL SHIRTS

30. FUR

31. G-STRING

32. GLITTER

33. GLOVES

34. HAND PUPPETS

35. HATS

36. HOOKED RUG

37. HUMAN HAIR

38. JEANS

39. JEWELRY

40. KEY RING ORNAMENTS

41. KEYS

42. LABELS FROM CANS AND BOXES OF FOOD

43. LACE

44. LAMÉ

45. LEATHER

46. LOTTERY TICKETS

47. MARDI GRAS MASKS

48. MERIT BADGES

49. MINK STOLE

50. 100-YEAR-OLD QUILT

51. PASSPORT

52. PEARLS

53. PHOTOGRAPHS

54. PILLOWCASE

55. PINS

56. PLASTIC

57. RACING SILKS

58. RECORDS

59. RHINESTONES

60. ROPE

61. RUBBER THONGS

62. RUNNING SHORTS

63. SEQUINS

64. SHIRTS

65. SILK

66. SOCIAL SECURITY CARD

67. STUDS

68. STUFFED ANIMALS

69. SUEDE

70. SUIT JACKETS

71. T-SHIRTS

72. TAFFETA

73. TOYS

74. TUXEDO

75. VESTS

76. VINYL

77. WEDDING RINGS

78. WOODEN FLUTE

THE SPICE OF LIFE

10 NUNS

1. BENEDETTA CARLINI

Through a remarkable combination of good luck and hard work, modern historian Judith Brown uncovered the story of Benedetta, a nun born in the Tuscan mountains of Renaissance Italy in 1590. Surviving documents explicitly describe the nun's sexual relationship with another nun, and Brown tells the full story in her book *Immodest Acts*. Benedetta's secret was first discovered within her own lifetime, however, and she spent her last thirty-five years in prison.

2. VIRGINIA APUZZO

When she entered a convent at the age of twenty-six, Apuzzo had already been in two relationships, but wanted time to "think about what to do with my life." In 1982, long out of the convent, she took the reins of the embattled National Gay Task Force and built it into the country's strongest national lesbian and gay organization.

3. MARY KREGAR

Kregar entered the Our Lady of the Sea Church in Port Isabel, Texas, in 1983. The next year, according to a lawsuit filed by an aggrieved husband, Kregar "seduced" a married woman and broke up a twelve-year marriage. A jury agreed, and in 1988 awarded the husband $1.5 million in damages.

4. JEANNE CORDOVA

Cordova's reasons for entering the Immaculate Heart of Mary order in the 1960s weren't entirely spiritual: She had a crush on one of the nuns. When that chapter of her life ended, she became an early lesbian activist. Cordova co-founded the Lesbian Center in Los Angeles, and published *The Lesbian Tide*. Her book *Kicking the Habit* tells more.

5. MARGE HELENCHILD

She entered a convent as a way to escape from a difficult

home life, but Helenchild soon found existence as a nun to be too regimented. She left the order and played tackle for a women's pro football team, then co-founded the Radical, Lesbian, Feminist, Terrorist Comedy Group.

6. DIANA DiPRIMA
DiPrima entered a convent in 1960, but was alarmed at what she had to endure: Every Saturday evening, she and other nuns had to gather in the chapel and whip themselves or one another to atone for the sins of people who were out of town. DiPrima left after only eighteen months.

7. MARY MENDOLA
Mendola was a newswriter in the WACs, then a nun, before she embarked on her writing career. She is best known today as the author of *The Mendola Report,* a far-reaching look at gay and lesbian couples.

8. JEAN O'LEARY
Soon after graduating from high school, O'Leary entered a convent. At the time, she thought she had a religious calling. But she had eight lesbian relationships while in the convent, and later realized that her entrance to it had much to do with her lesbianism. O'Leary later became executive director of the National Gay Rights Advocates.

9 & 10. ROSEMARY CURB and NANCY MANAHAN
Curb and Manahan compiled the controversial anthology *Lesbian Nuns: Breaking Silence,* which gave new visibility to the existence of lesbians in the convent. In the U.S., the book became the focus of much angry debate within the lesbian community when the lesbian publisher, Naiad Press, sold excerpt rights to *Forum* magazine. The controversy continued overseas: During a book tour in Ireland, the co-editors were thrown out of their Dublin hotel room after appearing on television. Sales skyrocketed.

THE 12 MEMBERS OF
THE FURIES COLLECTIVE,
AND WHERE THEY ARE NOW

One of the most active lesbian organizations of the early 1970s was The Furies, a group based in Washington, D.C., and made up largely of feminists who, because of their lesbianism, were excluded from more mainstream women's organizations.

1. GINNY BERSON

She is now a writer and radio producer. After The Furies dissolved she helped found Olivia Records, where she worked until 1980. She ran a concert production company called Heart's Desire for a few years, then went to work at KPFA radio in Berkeley until 1990, becoming director of women's programming, then program director. She is still a lesbian and has become a fanatic scuba diver. After all these years she finds she is still impressed with The Furies' "excellent analysis" (of heterosexuality, etc.) but says she herself has lost that old "fuck-you" stance.

2. JOAN E. BIREN

Joan Biren is better known as the photographer JEB. In the 1970s, she worked as a commercial free-lance photographer and with Moonforce Media, a feminist film distribution company. Since publishing *Eye to Eye: Portraits of Lesbians* in 1979, she has supported herself as a lesbian photographer, and for much of the 1980s she traveled with multimedia slide shows of her work, most recently *For Love and for Life: The 1987 March on Washington for Lesbian and Gay Rights.* She published a second book, *Making a Way: Lesbians Out Front,* in 1987. She is now working in video production, having revived Moonforce Media as a video production company.

3. RITA MAE BROWN

Since *Rubyfruit Jungle,* Brown has published six other novels (most recently, *Bingo*) and a nonfiction book on writing, *Start-*

ing from Scratch. Living hand-to-mouth in the mid-1970s while she wrote *In Her Day* and *Six of One* — at least until she got an NEA grant — Brown then supported herself for a time writing screenplays and teleplays, including *The Long Hot Summer.* She moved to California in 1981 to work for Norman Lear on the TV show *I Love Liberty,* for which she won an Emmy nomination — her second — and in 1982 won the Writers Guild's America Award for the best variety show. She also moved back to Charlottesville, Virginia, in 1982, where she continues to live and write.

4. CHARLOTTE BUNCH

After The Furies disbanded, Bunch helped found *Quest: A Feminist Quarterly,* then became a consultant with the National Gay Task Force. She has edited several books, including three collections of essays from The Furies and, with Sandra Pollack, a collection of essays on feminist education, *Learning Our Way.* Her own essays have been collected in the book *Passionate Politics,* which spans nearly twenty years and includes a summary of the many projects she has been involved in over the years. Bunch remains an ardent activist and organizer in the global feminist movement and is currently director of the Center for Global Issues and Women's Leadership at Rutgers University.

5. SHARON DEEVEY

Deevey has been a nurse for ten years as well as pursuing academic work: Her master's thesis examined lesbians over fifty. Currently a doctoral student at Ohio State University, where she is doing research on lesbian health, she is also a frequent public speaker on nursing issues related to gay and lesbian patients. She continues to stay in touch with other Furies members.

6. HELAINE HARRIS

Harris went on to co-found Olivia Records (with other Furies members, including Ginny Berson). In 1974 she co-founded Women in Distribution to help women's presses get wider circulation for their books. She is now vice president at Daedalus, a book remainder company with an emphasis on literary titles.

7. SUSAN HATHAWAY

Other Furies members have lost touch with Hathaway, but she is rumored to be married and a born-again Christian.

8. NANCY MYRON

Myron worked briefly at Diana Press, then moved to Washington, D.C., to work as a graphic designer. Since 1979, she and Charlotte Bunch have shared a Brooklyn apartment, and for the last eight years she has worked as a caterer, running her own business, Tables Catering, since 1985. She continues to support various local lesbian and gay endeavors as a volunteer.

9. TASHA PETERSON

At last report she was living in upstate New York.

10. COLETTA REID

Reid went directly from The Furies to Diana Press, where she worked for ten years. (Among the titles published while she was there were the three Furies anthologies edited by Charlotte Bunch.) Reid then became a small-business consultant in Sante Fe, moving back to California after two years to become a manager at Apple Computers. For the past few years, she has been executive director of a nonprofit agency providing counseling to women recovering from alcoholism and drug abuse.

11. LEE SCHWING

At last report, Schwing had joined an ashram in India.

12. JENNIFER WOODHUL

Woodhul is no longer a lesbian. She has been married for four years and has three children, including one from a previous lesbian relationship. She lives in the mountains in California and works as a free-lance technical writer. She credits Alcoholics Anonymous with changing the course of her life and her relationship to activism.

22 PEOPLE FROM GAY COMMUNITY NEWS, AND THEIR LATER ACCOMPLISHMENTS

The Boston-based *Gay Community News* must hold a record for the number of staff members who have gone on to make further contributions to the lesbian and gay community. They include:

1. BOB ANDREWS
   GCN board member; became founding member of the AIDS Action Committee of Massachusetts.

2. MICHAEL BRONSKI
   Has been *GCN*s lead features writer for over a decade; wrote *Culture Clash: The Making of Gay Sensibility.*

3. RICHARD BURNS
   GCN managing editor and president of the board. Later was the founding president of GLAD (Gay and Lesbian Advocates and Defenders) from 1978 to 1986, and is executive director of the Lesbian and Gay Community Services Center in New York.

4. KEVIN CATHCART
   GCN features editor; now executive director of Gay and Lesbian Advocates and Defenders.

5. BARRY FORBES
   GCN board member; became development director of the AIDS Action Council in Washington.

6. LOIE HAYES
   GCN features editor; now on the staff of South End Press, a progressive and feminist book publisher.

7. SUE HYDE
   GCN news editor; became the director of the National Gay and Lesbian Task Force's Privacy Project.

8. AMY HOFFMAN
   GCN features editor; also a co-founder of *Bad Attitude*.

9. JOE INTERRANTE
   GCN features writer; now head of the Health Issues Task Force, Cleveland's major AIDS organization.

10. IAN JOHNSON
    One of the earliest paid staffers at *GCN*; became active in neighborhood organizing and the editor of Boston's gay newspaper, *Bay Windows*.

11. TIM McFEELEY
    GCN volunteer writer; now executive director of the Human Rights Campaign Fund.

12. NEIL MILLER
    GCN news editor and managing editor; later wrote *In Search of Gay America*.

13. CINDY PATTON
    GCN features editor and managing editor; became president of the AIDS Action Committee; wrote *Sex and Germs: The Politics of AIDS*; and co-founded *Bad Attitude*, a lesbian sex magazine.

14. DAVID PETERSON
    GCN co-founder; later co-founded Boston's Gay Speakers Bureau.

15. BETSY RINGLE
    GCN fundraising volunteer; became a staff member of the National AIDS Network in Washington.

16. CINDY RIZZO
    GCN news and features writer and president of the board; later on the Gay and Lesbian Advocates and Defenders board, and now on the Capital Campaign staff of the Fenway Community Health Center.

17. ERIC ROFES

GCN features editor; became head of the beleaguered Gay and Lesbian Community Services Center in Los Angeles, which he is credited with reviving. Later became executive director of San Francisco's financially troubled Shanti Project. Also wrote *Socrates, Plato, and Guys Like Me,* a book about his experiences as a schoolteacher who came out.

18. HARRY SENG

GCN managing editor; later became news editor at *The Advocate.*

19. LAURIE SHERMAN

GCN ad manager and managing editor; now in charge of AIDS education at the AIDS Action Committee of Massachusetts.

20. TIM SWEENEY

GCN marketing and promotions volunteer; became head of Lambda Legal Defense and Education Fund, and later of Gay Men's Health Crisis.

21. URVASHI VAID

GCN features editor; now executive director of the National Gay and Lesbian Task Force.

22. JOHN WARD

GCN's volunteer attorney; became the first volunteer executive director in 1978 of Gay and Lesbian Advocates and Defenders.

4 POPULAR BIRTHDAYS

1. FEBRUARY 6
   actor Ramon Novarro (1899)
   poet F.W.H. Myers (1843)
   writer John Henry Mackay (1864)
   historian Martin Duberman (1930)
   Queen Anne of England (1665)
   contemporary mystery writer Shelley Singer (1939)
   King Richard II of England (1367)

2. FEBRUARY 22
   writer Felice Picano (1944)
   activist and writer Karla Jay (1947)
   poet Edna St. Vincent Millay (1892)
   science fiction novelist Joanna Russ (1937)
   composer Frederic Chopin (1810)
   writer Jane Bowles (1917)
   Boy Scout founder R.S.S. Baden-Powell (1857)
   writer Lige Clark (1944)

3. APRIL 15
   writer Henry James (1843)
   NGLTF co-founder Dr. Howard Brown (1924)
   poet Bliss Carmen (1861)
   singer Bessie Smith (1894)
   jack-of-all-trades Leonardo da Vinci (1452)
   activist and writer Sally Gearhart (1931)

4. AUGUST 1
   novelist Herman Melville (1819)
   poet Stuart Merrill (1863)
   poet Walter Griffin (1937)
   Roman emperor Claudius I (10 B.C.)
   novelist Radclyffe Hall (1883)
   fashion designer Yves St. Laurent (1936)

27 WAYS TO DIE

1. CRUCIFIXION: Polycrates (c.522 B.C.), *Samoan dictator*

2. POISON HEMLOCK: Socrates (469–399 B.C.), *Greek philosopher*

3. ASSASSINATED BY SUPPOSED FRIENDS: Julius Caesar (100–44 B.C.), *Roman ruler*

4. AN ARROW IN THE BACK: William Rufus (1060?–1100), *English king*

5. BEHEADED WITH LOVER: Conradin (1252–1268), *Hohenstaufen prince*

6. RED-HOT POKER THRUST UP THE RECTUM: Edward II (1284–1327), *English king*

7. LAUGHING AT A DIRTY JOKE: Pietro Aretino (1492–1556), *English dramatist*

8. GUILLOTINE: Robespierre (1758–1794), *French revolutionary*

9. IN A DUEL: Alexander Hamilton (1757–1804), *U.S. statesman*

10. HANGED AS A TRAITOR: Roger Casement (1864–1916), *Irish patriot*

11. BLOWN UP BY A MINE: Horatio Herbert Kitchener (1850–1916), *English general*

12. SUICIDE: Sir HECTOR MacDONALD (1853–1903). *British general*
MacDonald rose through the ranks from private to general, serving in India, Afghanistan, and Egypt (under Gen. Kitchener). After being made commander of the troops in Sri Lanka in 1902, he was accused of committing a "habitual crime of misbehavior with several schoolboys" and shot himself in the head when the allegation hit the European newspapers.

13. DOUBLE SUICIDE WITH LOVER: Michael Barrie and Rupert Buxton (d. 1915), *Oxford students*
Michael was one of the Barrie Boys who served as the inspira-

tion for *Peter Pan*. When he and his best friend drowned in a pool near Oxford, it was ruled an accident but many friends felt otherwise.

14. IN A CAR CRASH CAUSED BY PERFORMING FELLATIO ON THE CHAFFEUR: F.W. Murnau (1889–1931), *German film director*

15. FIRING SQUAD: Federico García Lorca (1898–1936), *Spanish poet*

16. LOST AT SEA IN A CHINESE JUNK: Richard Halliburton (1900–1939), *U.S. adventurer*

17. BITING INTO AN APPLE DIPPED INTO CYANIDE: Alan Turing (1912–1954), *British computer scientist*
By breaking a critical German code, Turing played a critical role in stopping Hitler's forces. England repaid him by arresting him for indecent behavior and forcing him to undergo hormone treatments that left him severely depressed. Turing's death is believed to have been a suicide, but he set it up so that his elderly mother could think — as she firmly did — that he accidentally got the poison onto his hands while performing an experiment.

18. PLANE CRASH: Dag Hammarskjold (1905–1961), *U.N. secretary-general*

19. MURDERED BY A JEALOUS LOVER: Joe Orton (1933–1967), *British playwright*

20. MURDERED BY A HUSTLER: Marc Blitzstein (1905–1968), *U.S. composer*

21. MURDERED BY TWO HUSTLERS WHO ARE BROTHERS: Ramon Novarro (1899–1968), *U.S. actor*
According to a widely circulated rumor, the murder weapon was a lead dildo that had been a present from Rudolph Valentino.

22. PUBLIC SUICIDE AND DISEMBOWELMENT: Yukio Mishima (1925–1970), *Japanese novelist*

23. OLD AGE: Natalie Barney (1876–1972), *French–American socialite*

Ramon Novarro, MGM's second Latin lover, was Rudolph Valentino's successor in more than one sense. His homosexuality was confirmed when, in his late sixties, he was murdered by two hustlers.

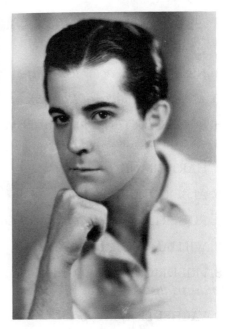

24. JEALOUSY: Veronica (Mabel) Batten (1857–1916), *British musician*

Batten and Radclyffe Hall had been lovers for eight years when hall met, and fell in love with, Una Troubridge. They argued violently about the new woman, then Batten — already in failing heath — dropped dead.

25. ALCOHOLISM AND DRUG ABUSE: Montgomery Clift (1920–1966), *U.S. actor*

26. MURDERED BY A ROBBER: Sal Mineo, (1939–1976), *U.S. actor*

27. JOY: Josephine Baker (1906–1975), *French–American entertainer*

In 1975, after many years away from the stage, Baker gave a sensational farewell performance. She fell asleep reading the ecstatic reviews, and never woke up. Friends swore that she died of joy.

20 PEOPLE WHO COMMITTED SUICIDE

1. NICK ADAMS, *actor who played Ben in* No Time for Sergeants

2. ANTINOUS, *lover of Hadrian*

3. ROGER AUSTEN, *author of* Playing the Game: The Homosexual Novel in America

4. HART CRANE, *poet*

5. ALBERT DEKKER, *actor*

6. ROBERT HOWARD, *creator of Conan the Barbarian*

7. WILLIAM INGE, *playwright*

8. FRIEDRICH ALFRED KRUPP, *nineteenth-century German industrialist*

9. VACHEL LINDSAY, *poet*

10. F.O. MATTHIESSEN, *literary critic*

11. REEVES McCULLERS, *husband of Carson McCullers*

12. CHARLOTTE MEW, *poet*

13. MARIO MIELI, *Italian gay rights activist*

14. YUKIO MISHIMA, *Japanese novelist*

15. NERO, *dictator*

16. ALFRED REDL, *Austrian-Russian spy*

17. SARA TEASDALE, *poet*

18. RENEÉ VIVIEN, *writer; she killed herself at the age of thirty-two*

19. JAMES WHALE, *film director*

20. VIRGINIA WOOLF, *writer*

9 TRANSSEXUALS

1. HELIOGABALUS (205–222)
   This Roman emperor had an affair with his handsome charioteer, dressed in fine silks, and tried in vain to find a surgeon who could turn him into a woman.

2. RAE BOURBON
   A vaudeville comedian and female impersonator, Ray Bourbon became "Rae" in the 1950s, in one of the first sex-change surgeries. He immortalized the experience on the record album *Let Me Tell You about My Operation*.

3. JAN MORRIS
   Still a successful travel writer and journalist, Morris eloquently described her journey from James to Jan in the 1974 book *Conundrum*.

4. ERNEST ARON
   John Wojtowicz, Aron's lover, tried to rob a New York bank to get money for Aron's sex-change operation. He got caught but Aron got his operation — paid for with the advance that his lover got for film rights to the robbery story. The film was *Dog Day Afternoon*, starring Al Pacino as Wojtowicz.

5. MARIANNE HERSEGARD
   Born a girl, Hersegard successfully underwent sex-change surgery in 1973; was married, as a man, to a woman; and then found she couldn't cope with playing a male role. She went back to the surgeon and is now a woman again.

6. BETH ELLIOTT
   Elliott, a folksinger and then-preoperative transsexual, was invited to perform at a major lesbian conference in 1973. Her presence there raised heated controversy over whether transsexuals should be considered women. She was eventually allowed to perform as scheduled.

7. RENEE RICHARDS

As a male, Richards had been a prominent eye surgeon; after surgery, she became a tennis player and coach.

8. LESLIE ELAINE PEREZ

An ex-convict-turned-politician, Perez managed to secure enough votes to force a run-off for the chair of the Democratic party in Harris County, Texas. Her opponent? Ken Bentsen, Jr., nephew of Sen. Lloyd Bentsen.

9. TERRI POHRMAN

She came in second in her bid to become mayor of Yountville, California. A former professional female impersonator, Pohrman had promised to bring more levity to municipal government.

19 NOTABLE CROSS-DRESSERS

1. ST. PELAGIA

Wearing a man's hairshirt, she called herself *frater Pelagius monachus et eunuchus* — literally, brother Pelagius, monk and eunuch.

2. KING HENRI III of France (1551–1589)

He loved to wear elegant women's clothing, even at public events, and surrounded himself with young men who shared his tastes.

3. ELENA/ELENO DE CÉSPEDES

This woman of sixteenth-century Spain, who may have actually been a hermaphrodite, got married first as a woman and then as a man.

4. QUEEN CHRISTINA of Sweden (1626–1689)

When she was born, Christina was at first thought to be a boy, and there is still speculation that she may have been a hermaphrodite. She often wore men's clothes, and after abdicating the throne in 1654, lived for a time under the name "Count Dohna."

5. LORD CORNBURY (Edward Hyde) (1661–1723).
As colonial governor of New York and New Jersey, he spent each afternoon promenading about in women's clothing. He explained that he did this as a tribute to his cousin, Queen Anne, but no one believed him.

6. Chevalier CHARLES d'EON de BEAUMONT (1728–1810)
A French diplomat, he undertook confidential missions for his country while disguised as a woman.

7. CHARLOTTE CHARKE (eighteenth-century)
She wore male clothes from infancy and made her living on the English stage as a male impersonator; her biography was published in 1755.

8. NADEZHDA DUROVA (1783–1866)
This Russian woman left her government official husband and her three children to join the Cossacks in fighting the Napoleonic wars.

9. Dr. JAMES BARRY (1795–1865)
By posing as a young man, she became the first woman in Great Britain to earn a medical degree; she continued in that male identity for the rest of her life and rose to the position of senior inspector-general of the British Army Medical Department.

10. ELIZA EDWARDS (1814–1833)
This English actress and prostitute was discovered after death to have been a male transvestite.

11. OMAR KINGSLEY (1840–1879)
As Ella Zoyara, he was a famous American equestrian.

12. EMIL MARIO VACANO (1840–1892)

He appeared as an equestrian under various female names and was Austria's "most important and prolific writer on the circus."

13. TOM ROWLANDSON (early nineteenth-century)

A highwayman, Rowlandson dressed in women's clothes and demanded jewelry from his victims.

14. THAI MINISTER OF DEFENSE

In the 1970s this government official won a national contest for best female dresser.

15. WARREN HARPER

Harper showed up for his high school senior prom wearing a chiffon dress, fur cape, and satin pumps, on the arm of his tuxedoed escort — his sister, Florence. Officials at the Trenton, Ohio, school removed them from the dance, but his mother thought the publicity might help him: "He wants to be Miss Gay Ohio when he's twenty-one," she said. "After that he'd like to go on to Miss Gay USA.

16. JOSE SARRIA

A legend in San Francisco, Sarria — aka the Dowager Widow of the Emperor Norton, Empress of San Francisco, and Protectress of Mexico — was also the first openly gay person to run for political office in San Francisco. He got 6,000 votes in his 1961 bid to become supervisor.

17. FRANK MASCARI

He was arrested for leading a Long Island burglary ring dressed in drag. Local police officers consider Mascari, aka "Mascara," to have "exquisite taste."

18. CHARLES DAUGHERTY

At twenty-six, he enrolled at a Colorado Springs high school as "Cheyen Weatherly" — even joining the cheerleading squad.

He was arrested after eight days — and two pep rallies — for criminal impersonation and forgery.

19. ROBERTA CLOSE
Close, a Brazilian transvestite, appeared on the cover of several major Brazilian magazines, billed as "the model of the beauty of the Brazilian woman."

6 PLANTS AND FLOWERS HISTORICALLY ASSOCIATED WITH HOMOSEXUALITY

1. VIOLETS
The association of violets with lesbians may have begun with a poem by Sappho, in which she describes herself and a lover as wearing garlands of violets. Violets were also worn by men and women in sixteenth-century England to indicate that they did not intend to marry. Used as a symbol of lesbian love in the 1926 Broadway production of Edouard Bourdet's *The Captive* — one of the first major dramas to include a lesbian theme — the violet became associated with lesbians in the U.S. for several decades.

2. PANSY
In Shakespeare's *A Midsummer Night's Dream,* Puck gathers pansies, said to have the magical power to "make man or woman madly dote/Upon the next live creature that it sees" — man or woman. The flower's association with gay men dates from at least 1903 in the U.S.

3. CALAMUS
In Greek mythology Calamus, the lover of Carpus, was changed to a reed after his lover drowned. Walt Whitman titled the most homoerotic section of *Leaves of Grass* "Calamus."

4. LADSLOVE
Besides this plant's suggestive name, its sap is said to smell like semen.

5. HYACINTH
When Hyacinthus, a youth whom Apollo loved passionately, was accidently killed after being struck by a discus Apollo threw in sport, the grief-stricken god turned him into a purple flower.

6. ORCHID
The name of this flower comes from a Greek word meaning "testicles." Because of the resemblance between testicles and the bulbs of certain kinds of orchids, the ancient Greeks believed that orchids grew wherever a man's or animal's semen fell. The term *orchid-eater* was sometimes used in nineteenth-century erotica as a euphemism for a gay man, especially one who enjoyed fellatio, and the technical medical term for castration is still *orchidectomy.*

7 BIRDS HISTORICALLY ASSOCIATED WITH MALE HOMOSEXUALITY*

1. CHICKENS
The Latin word for chicken, *pullus,* was a term of endearment especially used for handsome boys; *pullarius,* literally "poulterer," meant "boystealer" or "pederast." Contemporary American slang parallels this usage in *chicken* and *chicken hawk.*

2. HENS
In contemporary Spanish slang *polla,* "hen," refers to the penis, in contrast to the English *cock.*

---

* This list is derived from the *Encyclopedia of Homosexuality.*

3. ROOSTERS

On ancient Greek vases, older male suitors are commonly shown presenting roosters to youths; cocks were also associated with Dionysis, the bisexual god of wine. In contrast, *capon,* a castrated rooster, was once American slang for an effeminate or homosexual man.

4. THE EAGLE

Zeus is sometimes depicted as taking the form of an eagle to kidnap Ganymede.

5. PARTRIDGES

The readiness of the highly sexed male partridge to turn to another male as easily as to a female made a pair of male partridges a symbol for homosexual lust in classical writing.

6. RAVENS

The Roman satirical poets Martial and Juvenal depicted fellators as ravens, playing off of an ancient folkloric belief that ravens conceived through their beaks.

7. THE IBIS

The ibis's reputation for using its long beak to clean its own bowels led to its association with anal sex.

SAM STEWARD'S FEES FOR TATTOO TALK

In the early 1950s, Samuel Steward became, in all likelihood, the first person in history to abandon a career as a university professor for one as a tattoo artist. By all accounts, he was among the best. He later switched careers again to become a writer, using both his real name and the pseudonym Phil Andros.

In his new book *Bad Boys and Tough Tattoos,* Steward recalls life in his Chicago gallery. When he grew tired of hearing the same questions from customers again and again, he recalls, "I lettered a price list for them as a gag. Unfortunately, all too many visitors to the shop took it seriously."

1. For using the shop as a meeting place: $ .50

2. For giving advice to the lovelorn: 1.00

3. For listening to tales of woe: .75

4. For ½ hour of good stimulating talk: 1.00

5. For silly questions about tattooing ... each: .35

6. For use of can without getting tattoo: .25

7. For making change for parking meters: .50

8. For giving directions: 1.00

9. For listening to other tattooers' bullshit: 2.50

10. For talking about women I've tattooed: .40

11. For listening to jokes about tattooed dongs: 3.50

12. For reading comic books without getting tattooed: .50

13. For talking about techniques of tattooing: 1.50

14. For cheering people up: 1.25

15. For "lending" people a buck: 3.00

16. For answering questions about the money I make: 4.00

17. For listening to ordinary garden-type bullshit: 1.00

18. For explaining how tattoos are removed: 1.50

19. For hearing "I'm bleeding like a stuck pig": 1.00

20. For miscellaneous irritation: 2.00

Virginia Woolf, writer and
Abysinnian prince at large, sans
turban and greasepaint.

12 THINGS YOU SHOULDN'T HAVE BELIEVED

1. "A COLLEAGUE OF SAPPHO WROTE *LES CHANSONS DE BILITIS.*"

This book of erotic prose poems, many of them lesbian, was supposedly written by a woman contemporary of Sappho and translated from the ancient Greek into French by Pierre Louÿs. But Louÿs himself wrote it, supplying a biography of the author and a bibliography and notes, for good measure. The book was among the most successful literary hoaxes of the nineteenth century. Among its fans was Natalie Barney, who became good friends with the real author; another tribute to the work is that the Daughters of Bilitis took its name from the title.

2. "HI, I'M THE EMPEROR OF ABYSSINIA AND I'D LIKE YOU TO MEET MY THREE PRINCES."

The H.M.S. *Dreadnought* was the British Navy's most formidable, most modern, and most secret man o' war. In 1910, it was docked at the port of Weymouth, in southern England.

Hoaxster Horace Cole had a friend send a telegram to the captain, notifying him that the emperor of Abyssinia was about to pay a royal visit. He then dressed Virginia Woolf, her brother Adrian, painter Duncan Grant, and two other accomplices in turbans and caftans, using greasepaint and artificial beards to round out the disguises.

The entourage boarded the ship and received a grand tour from the captain. Adrian acted as interpreter, "translating" the captain's explanations into Swahili and, when his acquaintance with that failed him, classical Greek, à la Virgil. So thorough was the hoodwinking that Adrian and Virginia even managed to shake hands with a cousin serving on board without his recognizing them.

Cole later went to the British press with the story, much to the humiliation of the Navy.

3. "HI, I'M ... ER ... RICK MAE BROWN, AND I'D LIKE TO..."

Lesbian-feminist Rita Mae Brown went undercover in 1975 to spend an evening in the Club Baths in New York City. With the help of a gay male friend, she donned a fake mustache and a codpiece, adopted a butch stride, and, once inside, wore a bathrobe to cover her breasts. When unwanted hands meandered toward her crotch, she politely said no.

What did she learn? In an account of her adventure published in the weekly *Real Paper,* she observed, "The easiness of refusal is incredible... If you say 'no' it means 'no,' that's all... Sex isn't a weapon here, it's a release." And what about a lesbian bathhouse? "Our Xanadu would be less competitive than the gay men's baths, more laughter would ring in the sauna, and you'd touch not only to fuck but just to touch."

4. "HI, I'M LAUD HUMPHREYS AND I JUST STOPPED IN TO TAKE A LEAK."

Sociologist Laud Humphreys spent two years, in the late 1960s, studying the impersonal gay sex that takes place in selected restrooms. His technique was simple: While pretending to simply use the facilities, he took down the license numbers of men who stopped. He used that information to identify the men, then sought them out at their homes to conduct his interviews. Fifty-four percent, he found, were married men living with their wives.

Humphreys published his findings in *Tearoom Trade,* a book that was widely praised by both mainstream and gay critics despite its unusual subject matter. Years later, Humphreys himself came out.

5. "I'M SELLING TICKETS TO THE LAVENDER WORLD'S FAIR."

Billed as a huge carnival, the 1976 Lavender World's Fair was instead a huge fiasco. Six to eight thousand people showed up at the Los Angeles County Fairgrounds on Easter weekend, but when the fair's headliners, the Pointer Sisters, arrived and were not paid, they turned around and left without performing. The angry audience stormed the promoters' trailer. One promoter began refunding ticket money to a few people, then fled in a black limousine. Many more employees and entertainers were stiffed, and thousands of unhappy ticket holders were left with no show. Most laughable about the whole affair was that the promoters — whatever their plans may have been — barely broke even on the fraud.

6. "THERE'S A SEX AND DRUG RING ON CAPITOL HILL."

In the summer of 1982, the headlines sizzled with stories about a sex and drug ring involving members of Congress and the high-school interns who serve as Capitol Hill pages. The episode began when NBC aired allegations that the nation's security was being endangered by homosexuals in Washington; as evidence, they quoted an unnamed callboy who claimed to have clients in Congress and the Pentagon. House page Leroy Williams then provided similar testimony, and ABC found another unidentified callboy to testify.

By summer's end, the bubble had burst. The two anonymous callboys turned out to be paid FBI informants. Williams was termed "a pathological liar" by co-workers, and eventually admitted he had lied. There is no evidence that the events that were so widely charged to have happened ever took place.

7. "THE POST OFFICE IS COMPILING A LIST OF PEOPLE WHO
WANT TO GET SEXUALLY EXPLICIT MATERIAL."

Well, no, actually the list compiled in 1971 was of people who
didn't want to get sexually explicit material, and 6,700 said they
didn't. But, wrote *San Francisco Chronicle* columnist Herb Caen,
32,000 misunderstood and asked to be placed on a list to *receive*
such mailings.

8. "A HOMOSEXUAL SPY RING HAS INFILTRATED THE
BRITISH ROYAL AIR FORCE."

In 1985 Royal Air Force investigators accused seven servicemen of operating a "homosexual spy ring" at a top secret
radio post on Cyprus. The seven, who had confessed to selling
secrets to gay Russian agents "by the bagful," were reportedly
blackmailed into doing so after attending a series of homosexual
orgies.

Their trial was the longest and most costly espionage trial in
British history. Testimony soon made it clear that British military
police had tortured the servicemen into confessing. They had
been kept awake for weeks, forced to hold heavy objects in the
air for hours, denied access to the toilet, and questioned for days
without an attorney. One serviceman attempted suicide twice
during the interrogations.

It was further revealed that there were, in fact, no Russians —
the "KGB major" turned out to be a local policeman. In addition,
several of the defendants weren't even in Cyprus when the "spy
ring" was allegedly operating. All seven servicemen were acquitted on all counts, and the British government was roundly
condemned by Parliament members from all parties.

9. "GM SEEKS SAME..."

A vicious 1987 scam victimized at least fifteen gay men in the
Chicago area. Respondents to an innocuous-sounding personal
ad in an alternative newspaper were shocked when, a few
months later, their employers, colleagues, landlords, and neighbors received letters identifying them as homosexuals and potential AIDS carriers and concluding with the warning "AVOID THIS
HOMOSEXUAL AT ALL COSTS."

The letters were sent by a group calling itself the "Great White Brotherhood of the Iron Fist," which claimed to seek the "complete ruination of homosexuality."

10. "A LOVESICK GAY SAILOR BLEW UP THE *IOWA*."
When a gun turret blew up on the battleship U.S.S. *Iowa* in 1989, Navy investigators flatly ruled out the possibility that it was an accident. Instead, they were quick to point a finger at Gunner's Mate Clayton M. Hartwig. Characterizing Hartwig as an introverted "loner" and a homosexual, they suggested that he deliberately set off the blast as an act of unrequited love for another sailor.

The investigation was later reopened under congressional prodding. Scientists discovered that pressure in the turret could well have been enough to detonate its gunpowder. Although the cause of the explosion could not be firmly established, there was no good reason to conclude that Hartwig had done it.

11. "SKINHEADS BEAT ME UP."
In July of 1989, Lynn Griffis, an assistant pastor at San Francisco's Metropolitan Community Church, reported that she had been beaten, kidnapped, and raped by skinheads on two separate occasions. Local activists organized protests to call attention to anti-gay violence, self-defense classes were organized, and the city offered a $10,000 reward for leads in the case.

Within a month, Griffis's story had come under suspicion. The San Francisco medical examiner concluded that her injuries were self-inflicted, and physical evidence taken at the scene of the alleged crimes contradicted her testimony. Griffis eventually asked the police to stop investigating "so that healing can occur," and she left town. Activists worried that the apparently false reports would distract attention from actual gay-bashings.

12. "THE TAX COLLECTOR WOULD LIKE TO SEE YOUR DOCUMENTATION."
Los Angeles City Councilman Joel Wachs could only listen to tax hearings for so long before his mind started to wander. Pretty soon he had devised a new revenue enhancer: A penis tax. He

wrote it up as an official-looking resolution, purportedly from the council's Revenue and Taxation Committee.

Like most good taxes, Wachs's was progressive: "Ten to twelve inches: luxury tax. Eight to ten inches: pole tax. Six to eight inches: privilege tax. Four to six inches: nuisance tax. Anyone under four inches is eligible for a refund. Please do not request an extension."

When other members of the council expressed dismay at their colleague's sense of humor, he responded, "All I wanted to do was liven up this dull scene at City Hall."

BIBLIOGRAPHY

Ackroyd, Peter. *Dressing Up: Transvestism and Drag: The History of an Obsession.* London: Thames & Hudson, 1979.

Advocate. 1967–present.

Bell, Quentin. *Virginia Woolf: A Biography.* New York: Harcourt Brace Jovanovich, 1972.

Brown, Rita Mae. *Starting from Scratch.* New York: Bantam, 1988.

Bunch, Charlotte. *Passionate Politics: Feminist Theory in Action.* New York: St. Martin's, 1987.

Cavin, Susan. *Lesbian Origins.* San Francisco: Ism Press, 1985

D'Emilio, John. *Sexual Politics, Sexual Communities: The Making of a Homosexual Minority in the United States, 1940-1970.* Chicago: University of Chicago Press, 1983.

Duberman, Martin Bauml; Vicinus, Martha; and Chauncey, George, Jr., eds. *Hidden from History: Reclaiming the Gay and Lesbian Past.* New York: New American Library, 1989.

Dynes, Wayne R., ed. *Encyclopedia of Homosexuality,* 2 vols. New York: Garland, 1990.

Foster, Jeanette H. *Sex Variant Women in Literature.* Tallahassee, Fla.: Naiad, 1985.

Gayellow Pages: The National Edition, 1991. New York: Renaissance House, 1990.

Grahn, Judy. *Another Mother Tongue: Gay Words, Gay Worlds.* Boston: Beacon Press, 1984.

Greif, Martin. *The Gay Book of Days.* Secaucus, N.J.: Lyle Stuart, 1982.

Katz, Jonathan Ned. *Gay/Lesbian Almanac: A New Documentary.* New York: Harper & Row, 1983.

————. *Gay American History: Lesbians and Gay Men in the U.S.A.* New York: Harper & Row, 1976.

Malinowsky, H. Robert, comp. *International Directory of Gay and Lesbian Periodicals.* Phoenix: Oryx Press, 1987.

Morse, Carl; and Larkin, Joan, eds. *Gay and Lesbian Poetry in Our Time.* New York: St. Martin's, 1988.

Rodgers, Bruce. *Gay Talk: A (Sometimes Outrageous) Dictionary of Gay Slang.* New York: Putnam's, 1972.

Tripp, C.A. *The Homosexual Matrix.* New York: McGraw-Hill, 1975.

Weiss, Andrea; and Schiller, Greta. *Before Stonewall: The Making of a Gay and Lesbian Community.* Tallahassee, Fla.: Naiad, 1988.

Wickes, George. *The Amazon of Letters: The Life and Loves of Natalie Barney.* London: W.H. Allen, 1977.

World of Winners, 1st ed. Detroit: Gale Research, 1989.

INDEX

Also available from
Alyson Publications

THE ALYSON ALMANAC, by Alyson Publications staff, $9.00. Almanacs have been popular sources of information since "Poor Richard" first put his thoughts on paper and Yankee farmers started forecasting the weather. Here is an almanac for gay and lesbian readers that follows these traditions. You'll find the voting records of members of Congress on gay issues, practical tips on financial planning for same-sex couples, an outline of the five stages of a gay relationship, and much, much more.

THE GAY BOOK OF LISTS, by Leigh Rutledge, $8.00. Rutledge has compiled a fascinating and informative collection of lists. His subject matter ranges from history (6 gay popes) to politics (9 perfectly disgusting reactions to AIDS) to entertainment (12 examples of gays on network television) to humor (9 Victorian "cures" for masturbation). Learning about gay culture and history has never been so much fun.

LESBIAN LISTS, by Dell Richards, $9.00. Lesbian holy days is just one of the hundreds of lists of clever and enlightening lesbian trivia compiled by columnist Dell Richards. Fun facts like uppity women who were called lesbians (but probably weren't), banned lesbian books, lesbians who've passed as men, herbal aphrodisiacs, black lesbian entertainers, and switch-hitters are sure to amuse and make *Lesbian Lists* a great gift.

THE GAY FIRESIDE COMPANION, by Leigh Rutledge, $9.00. Leigh Rutledge, author of *The Gay Book of Lists,* has written fact-filled articles on scores of subjects: unusual gay historic sites in the U.S.; fascinating mothers of famous gay men; footnote gay people in history; public opinion polls on homosexuality over the last twenty years; a day-by-day, year-by-year history of the AIDS epidemic.

CRUSH, by Jane Futcher, $8.00. It wasn't easy fitting in at an exclusive girls' school like Huntington Hill. But in her senior year, Jinx finally felt as if she belonged. Lexie — beautiful, popular Lexie — wanted her for a friend. Jinx knew she had a big crush on Lexie, and she knew she had to do something to make it go away. But Lexie had other plans. And Lexie always got her way.

OUT OF ALL TIME, by Terry Boughner, $7.00. Historian Terry Boughner scans the centuries and picks out scores of the past's most celebrated gay, lesbian, and bisexual personalities. From ancient Egypt to the twentieth century, from Alcibiades to Willa Cather, we discover a part of history that has too often been censored or ignored. Each chapter is imaginatively illustrated by *Washington Blade* caricaturist Michael Willhoite.

MACHO SLUTS, by Pat Califia, $10.00. Pat Califia, the prolific lesbian author, has put together a stunning collection of her best erotic short fiction. She explores sexual fantasy and adventure in previously taboo territory — incest, sex with a thirteen-year-old girl, a lesbian's encounter with two cops, a gay man who loves to dominate dominant men, as well as various S/M and "vanilla" scenes.

Ask for these titles in your favorite bookstore. Or, to order by mail, use this coupon or a photocopy.

- -

Enclosed is $_____ for the following books. (Add $1.00 postage when ordering just one book. If you order two or more, we'll pay the postage.)

1. _____

2. _____

3. _____

name: _____

address: _____

city: _____ state: _____ zip: _____

ALYSON PUBLICATIONS
Dept. H-82, 40 Plympton St., Boston, MA 02118

After June 30, 1992, please write for current catalog.